Pimp my RICE

Pimp my RICE

NISHA KATONA

NOURISH

EAT WELL, LIVE WELL

For my Maa, for Monmon, for India and for Tia – my alphas and my omegas

Pimp My Rice
Nisha Katona

First published in the UK and USA in 2015

This edition published in the UK and USA by
Nourish, an imprint of Watkins Media Limited
19 Cecil Court
London WC2N 4EZ
enquiries@nourishbooks.com

Publisher: Grace Cheetham
Managing Editor: Rebecca Woods
Editors: Wendy Hobson and Elinor Brett
Art Direction and Design: Georgina Hewitt
Production: Uzma Taj
Commissioned Photography: Lara Holmes
Cover Photography: Jon Ashford
Food Stylist: Aya Nishimura
Prop Stylist: Linda Berlin

A CIP record for this book is available from
the British Library

ISBN: 978-1-84899-325-5

10 9 8 7 6 5 4 3 2 1

Typeset in Gotham
Colour reproduction by XY Digital
Printed in China

Publisher's note:
While every care has been taken in compiling
the recipes for this book, Watkins Media
Limited, or any other persons who have
been involved in working on this publication,
cannot accept responsibility for any errors
or omissions, inadvertent or not, that may
be found in the recipes or text, nor for
any problems that may arise as a result
of preparing one of these recipes. If you
are pregnant or breastfeeding or have any
special dietary requirements or medical
conditions, it is advisable to consult a
medical professional before following any
of the recipes contained in this book.

Notes on the recipes:
Unless otherwise stated:
• Use organic produce, wherever possible
• Use medium eggs, fruit and vegetables
• Use fresh ingredients, including herbs
  and chillies
• Use unwaxed lemons
• Do not mix metric and imperial
  measurements
• 1 tsp = 5ml 1 tbsp = 15ml 1 cup = 240ml

nourishbooks.com

Contents

Introduction

'*Rice is the best, the most nutritive and unquestionably the most widespread staple in the world.*' Georges Auguste Escoffier (1846–1935)

The best staple in the world. Not just that, but the most nutritive and widespread staple in the world! That's how the renowned Escoffier described this wonderful grain. He didn't scoff so why do we?

The Indian rice phobe

I wrote this book because I felt rice needed to be celebrated. I think this is borne from my guilt. Guilt because, for years, I overlooked rice as an anodyne, pasty-faced accompaniment: always the bridesmaid, never the bride. Why in the West do we treat this grain of grains like a second-class citizen? Why is it relegated to the realms of lacklustre side orders? Why must we dress it in garish, clownish hues to justify its presence at the Indian feast? Why does its cooking technique continue to confound adults in the West when children in the East can cook it before they can pronounce it?

And I am as guilty as any. To be Indian and rice phobic is like being a vegetarian Turk: hobbled where it matters most – in your kitchen. I confess that I only learnt to master rice in my 30s, when I had a young family to cook for and little time to spare. Shame on me. I work full time as well as running a busy household, so I need ingredients that will be at my beck and call – grown-up ingredients that can be shown the dressings and trusted to work their own magic. Ingredients that need not be poked and prodded and peeled and goaded into a splendid main course. But I confess it was only once a young family eclipsed time that I learnt how to cook rice.

No stress, no straining

A story that changed my riceless life came from a friend who worked in Africa. There, with very limited fuel, she told me they used one cup of rice to two of water, boiled the pan once, then placed the pan in a polystyrene box and left it to cook by itself. It did so in 20 minutes. No heat, no stirring, no straining.

I became swollen with awe at this assiduous grain. I cannot think of another ingredient that requires so little, to give so much to so many.

Rice swells to three times its size when cooked. It is the staple food of over half the world's population. Its production alone keeps buoyant some of the world's poorest economies. Quick to cook and slow to burn, rice is patient, rice is kind, rice is not proud, rice does not boast ... biblical in its worthiness, I became a Rice Evangelist.

But it is not just because of these merits of rice that I wax so lyrical. It is because, quite selfishly, it allows me to cook quickly, spectacularly and deliciously with the least effort.

The world beyond British shores knows this. One-pot rice dishes are at the heart of the cuisines of the majority of the world's population. If one thinks of the crucible of rice – the kitchens of the East – this dedication makes sense. Rice cooking is favoured where fuel is precious, where pans are few, where mouths are many, where children sit on their mothers' hips as they cook one handed. It is in these lives that rice is understood to be a cook's best friend.

Since 2500BC our ancestors have known the simple importance of rice. And simple it is. I think many of us consider rice to be exotic, complicated, otherworldly. We think it is not our staple – our staples in the West are the potato, wheat and corn, none of which is as simple to prepare. I want to show you how to master the grain, to show you how rice is one of the hardest-working companions you can harness in your kitchen. It does not need peeling, it does not need chopping or endless preparation. It likes to be left to cook without a watchful gaze. It is eternally long-life if kept dry and airtight.

A spiritual heart

One of my first memories is sitting on my mother's knee while she mashed rice and delicately spiced fish between her fingers on a steel plate. Quickly, she formed small balls with which to feed me. I remember the glint of the stainless steel in the Skelmersdale sunshine, the deftness of her fingers and the speed and the purpose with which she gently pushed the morsel past my lips. This confident haste made the interaction somewhat non-negotiable. There are not many Asian babies who require the choo choo train spoon into the tunnel routine. For so many, including myself, it is rice that is the first taste of a mother's love.

And that continues. Indian life is punctuated by rice ceremonies. Almost in the form of a deity, rice is at the spiritual heart of so many life-affirming occasions. The weaning ceremony for children, known as the Annaprashan ceremony, involves the child taking its first solid food. And, of course, that solid is the mother of all Indian foods – boiled white rice.

When patients are at their weakest, the sustenance offered to them is often the cooking water of the rice, sometimes served like a soothing broth, lightly salted and with finely chopped onions. This was, in the mind of my mother, the panacea for all the gut rot I often suffered as a child on my voyages to India.

It is not uncommon for wedding ceremonies across both East and West to have an element of gratuitous tossing of rice grains. Rice is about fertility and this showering with hard carb pellets, it seems, does the world of good to the ovaries. In India, on entering the marital home for the first time, the new bride and groom make an offering of rice to the deities at the household shrine. The idea is that anything this good is bound to ward off bad spirits. Every little helps.

Even in death, the role of rice is not abated. On the first anniversary of a death, I recall observing a very touching ceremony involving rice balls. A huge ball of rice is formed to present to the household deities at the altar. This ball represents the life of the deceased. It is blessed and then broken into smaller balls. These represent the ancestors of the deceased. Each one is blessed in turn. A poignant image in my memory, rice balls of different sizes, representing the ancients, all stretched back in formation from their present son.

An international language

Rice is the grain of the East – sun and paddy fields create the environmental requirements. It needs little processing and preparation. There is no waste. There are infinite forms of the rice with which one can get inventive – grains, flour, roasted grains, rice paste, rice water.

Truth be told, I tired a little of the same musky pan of steamed basmati, day in, day out, growing up in an Indian home. I think this is what led me to travel the globe to see what others did by way of carb background noise. But I soon realized that – far from background noise – rice was often what was chosen as the stand-alone event.

In China, I was introduced to *cheung fun*, which is not just a dish for me now but an absolute addiction. Rice flour is formed into the most gelatinous, fat, sheets of silky tension. To me, the various fillings are incidental, a peripheral pleasure. The heart of the charm is the reluctant, sweet-sauced satin rice sheet. This was unrecognizable to me as rice. It was so wrong and yet so right. Indian food culture does not harbour these slippery, mollusk-like textures. It was a kind of rice adultery to me. Even now, if I take my mother for a dim sum feast, the *cheung fun* still poses a textural bridge too far. This is beyond rice, she says, with scorn.

I recall a steamy night market in Luang Prabang in Laos. A single, firefly-lit stall attracted a queue of locals, children with balls, willing to wait in the dark heat for whatever steamed enticingly into the black air. The pancake maestro created huge membrane-thin rice pancakes into which he drizzled layer upon layer of condensed milk, folding, folding, folding until he had warm, drooping envelopes of sweet Laotian love.

Tucked away in a covered fish market in Seogwipo in South Korea, I stumbled upon a lady who introduced me to the joy of spiced *tteok*, Korean rice cakes. They are called cakes but in shape they are huge, thick fingers of dense, soft rice noodle. This was cooked with angry-red spiced sauce. The clever counterpoint of the vicious sauce with the impenetrable, gentle density of the rice stick was almost therapeutic.

Rice noodles are coupled with the most extraordinary roast pork and light broth in the Vietnamese classic, *bun cha*. I travelled to Hanoi, Vietnam, for a cookery class. This dish was lesson one, and thereafter I enjoyed eating it day after day, sitting on the heaving pavements, on infant-size plastic stools. The Vietnamese not only know how to make rice noodles sing, I thought, their pensioners must also have crackingly good hips.

A surprising fondness for rice permeates throughout Europe and this is a fact that always startled me, as it is a continent that boasts a whole gamut of yeasty breads and pastas to savour. However, I began to understand the unique charm of rice as a tame and kindly stuffing when paired with minced/ground spiced pork in myriad Eastern European dishes. I get why a good Hungarian rice cake could only work when teamed up with the textured grit of the rice grain.

And when you savour the delights of the finest Italian risottos, you can't but think it was worth it. From an ignominious background noise in Italian peasant culture – brought over by the Arabs in the Middle Ages – the best risottos were often simply rice, stock and herbs. Once the centrepiece of frugality for the pastoral masses, it is some of these risottos that remain the most charming: risotto alla parmigiana and risi i bisi remain firm domestic favourites.

For rice has a different role in different continents. In the East it takes on almost divine importance, strutting in weird and wonderful forms, the life and soul of the table. The West subsumes it into a role of obedient foil, loyal accompaniment, quirky dessert jester. It took my globe-trotting greed to actively go and discover for myself how the grain is handled in the impenetrable covered markets, in the kitchens of grandmothers, and amidst the loud, colourful pavement stalls of the world.

I hail her now, as the most versatile ingredient on the planet. I simply want to share with you just some of the magical ways that the world wields its most incredible grain.

Cooking methods

There are 40,000 types of rice but – don't worry – I intend only to introduce you to the ones that are widely available. Basically, rice is classified mainly by the size of the grain. Long-grain rice is long and slender, staying separate and fluffy after cooking and thus making it a good absorbent side dish. Short-grain rice is shorter and plumper, those with a slightly longer grain working well in paella and risotto, while the short-grain pudding rices are almost round, with moist grains that stick together when cooked.

Each of these rices – and some other types, like red rice – has a feature in the book with details of how to cook it and an example recipe, so turn to the features for more information.

Brown rice (see page 24)
White basmati rice (see page 42)
Red rice (see page 52)
Sticky or glutinous rice (see page 64)
Sushi rice (see page 84)
Paella rice (see page 128)
Risotto rice (see page 146)
Wild rice (see page 172)
Pudding rice (see page 186)
Black rice (see page 214)

Each of the recipes in this book gives full instructions on how to prepare and cook the rice for that specific dish, but these pages will give you an overview of the principles of cooking rice to help you master the simple techniques.

To rinse or not to rinse

I was taught to rinse rice before cooking until the water runs almost clear. This can prove a ritual with many in the East. The rattle and slosh of rice being rinsed over and over is a lullaby to many children. There is no need. Rinse as you would your teacup and sing them a lullaby instead.

The theory goes that rinsing before cooking rice removes excess surface starch and so produces a whiter, cleaner-tasting dish. With long-grain rice this makes the final product more separate and less sticky. With sticky rice grains, it reduces – ever so slightly – the stick. Win win.

I have, rather obsessively, performed numerous taste tests on this theory and concluded that in terms of flavour the difference is zilch. There is a reduction in the white scum that can sometimes sit on white rice if it is not rinsed first, but that is the only difference my primitive palate could detect.

I confess, however – even in the face of all this starch evidence – I always rinse rice, just as I would always wash shop-bought fruit and veg: once or twice to wash away all unbidden traces of handlers.

To soak or not to soak

With the notable exception of a few recipes – mainly using brown rice – I rarely soak rice before cooking. But it is up to you if you have time. Soak in cold water for anything up to 3 hours. If you are cooking by the absorption method, cover with the measured amount of water (2 cups water to 1 cup rice), then cook without adding any more water.

For me, the beauty of rice is its humble, quick simplicity; soaking is a bridge too far. As a busy working mother, I generally eschew anything that is too needy in the kitchen, humans aside. I would rather use nuclear technology (okay, or a pressure cooker) on ingredients than tolerate the need to soak. It does not add enough to the dish to justify it. But if you feel it gives you a subtle edge and you have the time and patience, soak away. And here is why. Brace yourself.

It takes about 15 minutes for boiling water to reach the middle of a rice kernel, so while the outside has cooked for 15 minutes, the middle has been cooked for only a minute or so. And as the outside of the kernel cooks, starch leaches out, increasing stickiness.

Soaking white rice for about an hour before cooking allows moisture to get to the middle of the kernel. During cooking, the heat transfers quicker to the middle and the rice will be done in about eight minutes, causing less damage to the outside of the kernel. Thus it's more evenly cooked, and easier to separate than the non-soaked rice.

Season your grain offerings with salt (Leviticus 2:13)

I do add a pinch of salt to my rice because I love the stuff. I am a salt fiend.

However, it does not increase the boiling point of the water unless you are adding a shovel full. It will increase the fragrance of the rice a little and it also gives it an inevitably savoury edge. Apart from these optional benefits, it's not necessary at all, unless you feel your arteries need toughening up a little.

Useful rice-cooking tips

* One big mug of rice serves four hungry adults.
* Don't worry if you get a burnt crust on the bottom of the pan. In many countries, this is considered the best bit.
* If you agree and you want a burnt crust on the bottom, put the pan on a damp towel once the rice is cooked to help lift the crust off the pan.

* Avoid stirring the rice too much while it is cooking. This breaks the grains, releases starch and makes the rice sticky.
* Finished basmati rice should be as white as snow, smell a little of musk and have a slightly chalky interior.

The absorption method (my favourite)

This is the method for making 'steamed rice'. This method has a mindless simplicity. I discovered it when I was in my 30s – pretty late on in life for an Indian. It has never failed me. I fell in love with the kindness of rice after this – a cook's able helper, leaving you free to fret over other dishes. It almost brings the rice to life as the army of grains marshal and cook themselves, standing to a vertical phalanx of attention when cooked. It's all about what you don't do. It's about stepping away from the pan. It's my kind of cooking.

* For every one cup of rinsed rice, add 2 cups of water.
* Simmer until the water has almost all disappeared. This usually takes about 10–15 minutes. Stir once or twice in the early stages if you must.
* Then put on a tight lid, switch off the heat and wait for 15 minutes.
* Do not lift the lid before this precious 15-minute period has elapsed. The sealed pan becomes the kiln of the grain and it must not be disturbed.

The straining method

This was the method I grew up with. It was a two-parent job. Mother watched the pan, summoning my father away from the news to strain the heavy, boiling vat of terror. Accident and emergency stood poised. Most Indian families will have some relative with an elaborate burn scar from a rice-straining injury. But don't let me put you off. In the East, where one eye is always fixed on the blood sugar level, the straining method is believed best for diabetics. And every Indian family likes to boast at least one of those, too.

* Rinse the rice and add at least double the volume of water.
* Boil the rice for about 20 minutes, testing the grains frequently.
* When they are as soft as you want them, drain and rinse through with hot water. Remember that the rice will continue to cook slightly once back in the pan so don't wait until it is mushy before you strain it.

The finger method

The finger method has a natural charm to it as the body and the grain are working together. There's a total absence of any measuring implements, which is logical beacuse they rarely feature in the kitchens of the East, the crucible of rice cooking. It is basically the same principle as the absorption method, but without the mugs.

* Add as much rinsed rice as you like to any shape of pan.
* Add as much water as reaches to the first joint crease on your index finger when the tip of the finger is just touching the rice.
* Boil merrily until almost dry with a dimpled surface, about 20 minutes.
* Switch off the heat, add a tight lid and wait for 15 minutes.

The microwave method

This is my aunt's favoured method, and she is evangelical about cooking rice like this. 'It involves Pyrex, it's hands free – what's not to like?' she gushes. 'The fact that it is your idea,' says my mum.

* Use 2 cups of water for every cup of rinsed rice.
* Put in a large covered dish suitable for the microwave.
* Microwave in a 700watt oven until the grains stand dry and vertical, allowing 15 minutes per cup of rice.
* Remove and leave to rest for 5 crucial more minutes.

Using a rice cooker

Invented in 1937 by the Japanese army – a wooden box with two electrodes – the modern versions work on the principle of absorption but with equal quantities of rice and water. They are hailed by the majority of the world's population as indispensible, and so simple that many don't come with instructions. The benefits are that they cook the rice well, with minimum effort, and keep it warm. In households where rice is eaten daily and warm portions need to be ever ready, one can understand their importance.

For me, these machines always remind me of an episode of the UK television series *Father Ted*, a scene in which a crestfallen Mrs Doyle, houskeeper and keeper of the kettle, is given a TeasMaid for Christmas. Only the churlish can argue with the sense of these gadgets. I do tend to glaze over when I hear my Chinese friends expound their virtues. Truth be told, I know they are miraculously good machines but I do like to get my hands a little dirty. As Mrs Doyle says ... maybe I like the misery.

* Generally the instructions vary from model to model but it's roughly 1 cup rice to 1½ cups water, then you plug in and switch on while you switch off.

1

Kick starts

Blinged breakfasts

Banana espresso

Serves: 2
Prep: 2 minutes, plus chilling (optional)

Theories abound that both banana and coffee have notes of fragrant spice that suggest the aroma of cloves. That's the romantic justification for this recipe out of the way. Frankly, in terms of energy and stamina, coffee and banana are the Springer Spaniel and St Bernard of the kitchen. Hence this arranged-marriage smoothie should carry you, effortlessly, for miles and miles into your day.

- 1 banana, sliced
- 4 dried dates, pitted and chopped
- 4 shots cold espresso coffee
- 2 tsp caster/granulated sugar (optional)
- 400ml/14fl oz/1¾ cups rice milk
- a large pinch of ground cinnamon, for dusting (optional)

Put all the ingredients except the cinnamon in a blender and blitz for 2 minutes until smooth. Transfer to the refrigerator until cold, if you prefer a chilled drink.

Pour into glasses and dust the top with cinnamon, if you are so inclined.

Yogberry mint milk

Serves: 2
Prep: 5 minutes, plus chilling (optional)

Fibre from the rice bran, protein and potassium from the banana, pink kindness from the strawberry and the wake-me-up, cleansing zing of the mint. It's what your mother would want you to start your day with ... unless she is a gin-loving, 40-a-day kind of lady ...

150g/5½oz/1½ cups fresh or
  frozen strawberries
2 bananas, sliced
100g/3½oz/scant ½ cup
  plain yogurt
1 heaped tbsp rice bran
100ml/3½fl oz/scant ½ cup
  skimmed milk or soy milk
1 tbsp lemon juice
1 small handful of mint leaves
1 tbsp clear honey

Put all the ingredients in a blender and blitz for 2 minutes until smooth. Transfer to the refrigerator until cold, if you prefer a chilled drink.

Pour into glasses and enjoy.

Roasted rice tea

Serves: 2
Prep: 5 minutes
Cook: 8 minutes

A Japanese favourite called *genmaicha* or 'dark rice tea', I like to think of it as popcorn tea, as that is where its flavour takes me. This recipe makes a couple of cups of tea, but you can roast the rice in whatever quantity you like, then cool it and store it in an airtight container to use whenever you like.

2 tbsp brown rice
2 tsp English Breakfast, or
  your preferred tea leaves

Spread the rice in a thin layer in a wide heavy-based frying pan. Dry-fry the grains over a medium heat, stirring and re-spreading them constantly so that they brown evenly. Make sure that they do not burn as this will make your tea bitter. The process should take just over 5 minutes.

Remove the pan from the heat and allow the rice to cool completely.

Add the roasted rice grains and the tea leaves to a pot of boiled water and allow to steep for 1–3 minutes, depending on how strong you like your tea. Strain, drink, be well.

Not just a chichi fad

The rice is no mere ornament in this tea. The fasting culture of Japan means this carb-by-stealth tea was stomach-lining sustenance. Known as 'the people's tea', the rice provided a two-pronged benefit. It added substance to tea, and reduced the need for expensive tea leaves. See, it's not just a chichi Soho Teahouse fad. It was bread and butter to the workers of Japan.

A bloodier and much more satisfying genesis for this drink tells of an ancient Japanese legend. A servant named Genmai was serving his master, a samurai warrior, some tea when a few grains of rice accidentally fell out of his pocket and into the pot. The warrior was so infuriated that his servant had ruined a perfectly good cup of tea that he chopped off his head. He decided to drink the cup of tea anyway and was swept away by the wonderful flavours. In honour of his poor servant, he insisted that this combination of tea and rice be served every morning and named it *genmaicha* (*cha* means tea in Japanese).

When roasting the rice you need to be careful to get an even brown to the grains. Any burnt grains will cause bitterness in the tea; under-roasting will leave the grains unyielding and truculent. The tea leaves you choose to add are entirely down to what you fancy at the time. It could be herbal or traditional tea leaves. Experiment, but do add the hugely antioxidant-packed rice grains. The total transformation of flavour and texture in the rice through this dry-roasting process always reminds me what unseen alchemical magic lies in the depths of this humble grain. I love rice.

Caramel berry blend

This is a berry-sweetened porridge made from a coconut-based congee. Congee is the beef tea of the East, the porridge version of motherly love. For many in the East, this blended congee has been the stuff of rib-sticking recuperation. The berries are a bright, tart European twist. In China, I enjoyed this with jackfruit – a mango/toffee flavoured fruit with a pineapple consistency. I remember thinking that it stood sophisticatedly proud of the congee, pretending not to know the humble porridge around it. Berries, I thought, bullied into the blend by a little blitzing, would be a much better match.

150g/5½oz/heaped 1 cup raspberries, plus 6 whole raspberries, to garnish

150g/5½oz/1½ cups strawberries, plus 3 halved strawberries, to garnish

1½ tbsp demerara or muscovado/soft brown sugar

1 tsp lemon juice

THE CONGEE

90g/3¼oz/½ cup Thai fragrant rice or short-grain rice soaked for 2–4 hours, rinsed and drained

650ml/22fl oz/2¾ cups coconut milk

2 tbsp caster/granulated sugar

a pinch of salt

Chop the raspberries and strawberries roughly into large chunks, reserving all the juices. Reserve a few pieces to decorate, then leave them all to one side.

For the congee, heat the rice, coconut milk, caster/granulated sugar and salt in a heavy-based saucepan over a medium-high heat. Once the rice begins to boil, reduce the heat to a gentle simmer, stirring occasionally, for about 10 minutes until you have a porridge consistency.

Meanwhile, put the raspberries, strawberries, dememera sugar and lemon juice in a shallow frying pan over a medium heat and stir for about 8 minutes until the fruit softens but still has some bite, and the juice thickens slightly. Don't let it go to a toffee-like consistency.

Now you can either stir the berry mix into the congee until the red juices just bleed a little into the congee, or blend them together using a stick/immersion blender.

Serve warm or cold in bowls, decorated with the reserved fruit.

The hot date congee

Brown, wholesome and fruity. All the kick you get from that late-night Swiss muesli fix but at the right time of the day. You can add a swirl of coconut milk at the end instead of the dollop of something fresher, like yogurt. You could even use half the amount of milk during the cooking process and top up with 125ml/4fl oz/½ cup of coconut milk. This makes the dish more luxurious, richer and adds a sunshine twist to your wholesome morning.

Serves: 4
Prep: 5 minutes, plus soaking
Cook: 20 minutes

130g/4½oz/1 cup whole hazelnuts
200g/7oz/heaped 1 cup short-grain brown rice, soaked for 2 hours, rinsed and drained
3 tbsp soft brown sugar
a pinch of salt
240ml/8fl oz/1 cup whole milk
¼ tsp ground cinnamon, plus extra for sprinkling
6 dried dates, pitted and chopped
4 tbsp Greek yogurt or crème fraîche

Toss the hazelnuts in a small frying pan over a medium-high heat until they brown evenly all over. Remove from the pan and leave to one side.

Combine the rice, sugar, salt, milk and cinnamon in a saucepan. Bring to the boil over a medium-high heat, stir well, then lower the heat to medium-low. Add the chopped dates and simmer, covered, for 10–15 minutes, stirring occasionally. You are looking for a thick porridge consistency. Cook, uncovered, for 2 more minutes.

Spoon into serving bowls and sprinkle with a few toasted hazelnuts. Add a dollop of good Greek yogurt with a little pinch of cinnamon sprinkled over the top.

Brown rice

Brown rice is the whole grain of rice that is unmilled. It therefore retains the germ and the outer layers that contain beneficial fats. This makes it both a more nutritious and more substantial grain but more perishable too, because the fats within the bran and germ can spoil. What use is that in the heat of the East, one may ask?

While brown rice can be shunned in hotter climes, in the cooler kitchens of Europe it has enjoyed something of a renaissance. It pairs stunningly with deep, sweet ingredients, for instance, in The Hot Date Congee (see page 22) and in The Happy Hippy (see opposite). Brown rice in all its wholesome virtuosity is superb as a breakfast kick start. Its unrefined sustenance has a long, slow burn and the nutty taste that it brings gives the caramel, fruity ingredients cooked alongside it so much more intensity.

In the way that the flavours of white rice are considered elegant and subtle, brown rice has a marauding quality: unashamedly flavourful and rich – and great for the bowels. This will forever be its stigma in the East, where it is considered a peasant grain, a grain for the poorly, a grain for the constipated. In the East, brown rice is to white rice, what jute bags are to plastic. Cool and conscientious in the West, an ignominious necessity in the East.

How to cook plain brown rice

* Use 1 cup of rice to 2 cups of water (190g/6¾oz rice to 480ml/16fl oz water).

* Put the rice in a colander and rinse under cold running water until the water runs clear. Cover with cold water and leave to soak for 2 hours, then drain.

* Put the rice in a saucepan and add the water. Bring to the boil, then boil vigorously for about 10-15 minutes, uncovered, until almost dry with a dimpled surface.

* Cover tightly, remove from the heat and leave to stand for a full 20 minutes.

* Fluff up the grains with a fork.

The happy hippy

I always imagine true hippies and good Presbyterians have a bowl of leftover, morally airtight, always-a-bridesmaid, brown rice in the refrigerator. For such as these, the morning breaks forth reward in the form of golden butter and dark sugar, which comes from puritanical surplus – a filthily sweet, rib-sticking bowl of breakfast joy.

300g/10½oz/heaped 1½ cups short-grain brown rice, soaked for 2 hours, rinsed and drained
a pinch of salt
160ml/5½fl oz/scant ¾ cup whole milk
1½ tbsp butter
3 tbsp muscovado/soft brown sugar, or to taste
a pinch of freshly grated nutmeg
2 handfuls of nuts or crisp rice cereal (optional)

To cook the rice, put the rice and salt in a heavy-based saucepan and add 600ml/21fl oz/generous 2½ cups water. Bring to the boil over a high heat, then turn the heat down to medium and simmer for 30 minutes until the grains have almost completely absorbed the water. Remove from the heat, clamp on a tight lid and leave for 10 minutes.

Transfer the rice to a wide-based wok and add the milk and butter. Bring to a simmer over a medium heat, stirring occasionally, until most of the liquid has evaporated.

Stir in the sugar and nutmeg and once this has melted into the rice, switch off the heat.

Serve sprinkled with your favourite nuts or even a handful of crisp rice cereal to give that beckoning breakfast bite.

Serves: 4
Prep: 5 minutes
Cook: 7 hours

Salted cinnamon overnight pudding

This is *teurgole*, a Normandy dish that was cooked in the slow, dying heat of bread ovens. It's as hospitable a breakfast treat for houseguests as can be. It's mindlessly simple to throw together: bang in the oven and bake overnight after a heavy evening. Set your oven timer and, come morning, see your guests stagger, bleary eyed, into the open arms of a creamy cinnamon rice pudding under that thick duvet of browned, caramelized skin.

1 litre/35fl oz/4⅓ cups
   whole milk
65g/2¼oz/⅓ cup pudding or
   risotto rice, such as Arborio,
   rinsed and drained
100g/3½oz/½ cup caster/
   granulated sugar
¼ tsp salt
1 tsp ground cinnamon

Preheat the oven to 70°C/150°F/Gas ¼ or its lowest setting.

Stir all the ingredients together in a large pudding basin.

Bake in the middle of the oven for about 7 hours undisturbed. When finished, the dish will have a good brown crust. Dig in and enjoy.

Samoa cocoa rice

Serves: 4
Prep: 5 minutes
Cook: 25 minutes

The Samoans, I bet, are not as svelte as the French. I can, however, imagine them smiling a lot more at the 8am mark. This dish is a beloved breakfast in Polynesia. It is called *koko alaisa* and is served with a thick slice of generously buttered white bread. I imagine it to be a grandparent/grandchild sleepover pay-off, as surely parents wouldn't indulge children like this before school. Having said that, if one looks at some of the crack chocolate breakfast artillery in our supermarkets, parents across the globe, it seems, will do anything for a quiet morning.

200g/7oz/heaped 1 cup sticky rice, rinsed and drained

90g/3¼oz/scant ½ cup caster/granulated sugar, plus extra to serve (optional)

¼ tsp salt

165ml/5¼fl oz/⅔ cup evaporated milk, plus 60 ml/2fl oz/¼ cup extra to serve (optional)

90g/3¼oz/scant 1 cup unsweetened cocoa powder

1 tbsp grated orange zest

Combine the rice, sugar and salt in a saucepan over a medium-high heat and add 480ml/16fl oz/2 cups boiling water. Bring to the boil, then stir in the evaporated milk. Lower the heat to medium-low and simmer, covered, for 10–15 minutes. Every few minutes, give it a stir and wait for the rice to be cooked through.

While the rice is cooking, whisk 4 tablespoons boiling water into the cocoa powder in a small bowl and add the grated orange zest.

Once the rice is cooked, stir the cocoa mixture into the rice and continue to cook, uncovered, over a medium-low heat for another 5 minutes until the cocoa has been absorbed into the porridge.

Sprinkle with extra sugar and serve with extra evaporated milk, if you like.

Ginger beer rhubarb rice

Ginger and rhubarb are both tart, self-absorbed ingredients. They are uncompromising in their natural state, but just administer a little honey, sugar and a cushion of creamed rice and all grimace is gone.

175g/6oz/scant 1 cup
   pudding rice, rinsed and
   drained
600ml/21fl oz/generous
   2½ cups whole milk
65g/2½oz/4½ tbsp butter,
   cut into pieces
115g/4oz/heaped ½ cup
   caster/granulated sugar
4 egg yolks
a pinch of salt

**THE RHUBARB & GINGER
BEER COMPÔTE**
360g/12¾oz fresh rhubarb
   stalks, cut into 3cm/
   1¼in pieces
125ml/4fl oz/½ cup good-
   quality ginger beer
2 tbsp clear honey
1 tsp grated lime zest
juice of ¼ lime

To make the compôte, put the rhubarb, ginger beer and honey in a heavy-based saucepan over a medium-high heat and bring to the boil. Turn the heat down to low and add the lime zest and juice. Simmer for about 10 minutes until the stalks become tender. Leave to one side.

Meanwhile, put the rice and milk in a heavy-based pan over a medium heat and bring to a simmer. Reduce the heat to very low and allow the rice to simmer, covered, for 20 minutes. It needs to become thick and creamy. Remove the pan from the heat and stir in the butter, sugar, egg yolks and salt. Mix well.

Divide the rice among serving bowls and to each one add a good dollop of the compôte into the creamy pudding.

Creole crunchies

Deep-fry yourself to a good start with these little Creole rice doughnuts – a special weekend treat or weekday supper... after a hard day's slog in the office chair.

Serves: 4
Prep: 20 minutes, plus standing
Cook: 30 minutes

115g/4oz/scant ⅔ cup pudding rice, rinsed and drained
450ml/16fl oz/scant 2 cups semi-skimmed milk
a pinch of salt
2 tbsp caster/granulated sugar
50g/1¾oz/heaped ⅓ cup plain/all-purpose flour
1½ tsp baking powder
½ tsp ground cinnamon
¼ tsp ground ginger
a pinch of freshly grated nutmeg
1 tsp grated lemon zest
2 eggs
sunflower oil, for deep-frying
icing sugar, for dusting
maple syrup, for drizzling

To cook the rice, put the rice, milk and 450ml/16fl oz/scant 2 cups water in a heavy-based saucepan over a medium heat. Add the salt and bring to the boil. Turn the heat down to low and simmer for 15–20 minutes until the rice grains to begin to soften.

Now add the sugar and stir gently. Remove the pan from the heat and put on a tightly fitting lid. Leave the pan to stand for 15 minutes, by which time the rice in the pan should have absorbed all the water.

Transfer the rice to a food processor or blender and add the flour, baking powder, ground spices, lemon zest and eggs. Blitz until the mixture becomes a thick, smooth batter.

Heat the oil for deep-frying in a wok so that it is just smoking. Take a scoop of the batter in a dessertspoon, then ease this off into the hot oil using a second spoon. Repeat so that around 5–6 fritters fry together in the pan. Turn them carefully and wait for them to turn a golden brown. This should take about 3 minutes.

Lift the fritters out of the pan using a slotted spoon and drain on paper towels. Keep the cooked fritters warm in a low oven while you fry the remaining fritters.

Dust the fritters with icing sugar and serve with drizzle of good-quality maple syrup.

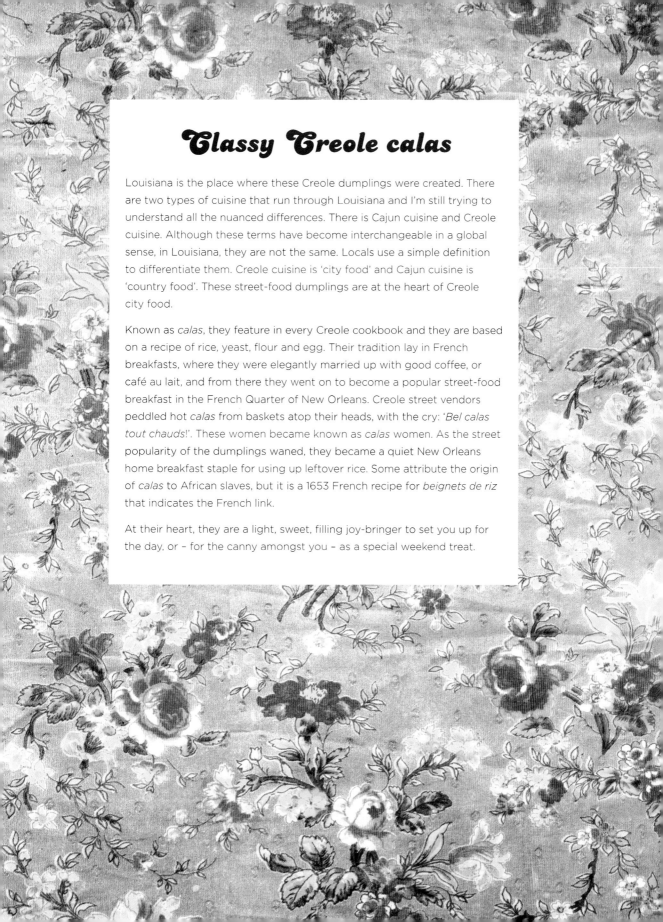

Classy Creole calas

Louisiana is the place where these Creole dumplings were created. There are two types of cuisine that run through Louisiana and I'm still trying to understand all the nuanced differences. There is Cajun cuisine and Creole cuisine. Although these terms have become interchangeable in a global sense, in Louisiana, they are not the same. Locals use a simple definition to differentiate them. Creole cuisine is 'city food' and Cajun cuisine is 'country food'. These street-food dumplings are at the heart of Creole city food.

Known as *calas*, they feature in every Creole cookbook and they are based on a recipe of rice, yeast, flour and egg. Their tradition lay in French breakfasts, where they were elegantly married up with good coffee, or café au lait, and from there they went on to become a popular street-food breakfast in the French Quarter of New Orleans. Creole street vendors peddled hot *calas* from baskets atop their heads, with the cry: '*Bel calas tout chauds*!'. These women became known as *calas* women. As the street popularity of the dumplings waned, they became a quiet New Orleans home breakfast staple for using up leftover rice. Some attribute the origin of *calas* to African slaves, but it is a 1653 French recipe for *beignets de riz* that indicates the French link.

At their heart, they are a light, sweet, filling joy-bringer to set you up for the day, or – for the canny amongst you – as a special weekend treat.

Red pecan pancakes

Serves: 4
Prep: 20 minutes
Cook: 1 hour

Paper-light pancakes filled with sweetened red rice and pecans. I have used the beautifully short Bhutanese red rice here, but this recipe works a treat with any red or brown short-grain rice. I love the rolled-up-sleeves attitude of the red grains. They are willing to give anything a go. Brisk in savouries, nutty in sweeter dishes. Okay, red rice takes a while to cook, but it freezes brilliantly.

175g/6oz/1⅓ cups plain/
    all-purpose flour, sifted
a pinch of salt
3 eggs
300ml/10½fl oz/generous
    1¼ cups milk mixed with
    100ml/3½fl oz/scant ½ cup
    water
80g/2¾oz/5½ tbsp butter
4 tbsp thick Greek yogurt

THE RICE & PECAN FILLING
1 tsp sunflower oil
50g/1¾oz/¼ cup red rice,
    preferably Bhutanese,
    rinsed and drained
75g/2½oz/¾ cup pecan nuts,
    roughly chopped
50g/1¾oz/¼ cup caster/
    granulated sugar
2 tbsp single/light cream
a pinch of ground cinnamon
1 tbsp sultanas/golden raisins
½ tsp vanilla extract
grated zest of ¼ lemon
1 tsp apricot jam

To make the filling, heat the oil in a large wok over a medium heat, add the rice and stir for 2 minutes. Turn up the heat, add 480ml/16fl oz/2 cups water and bring to the boil. Turn the heat down and simmer gently, covered, for 45 minutes or until the liquid has been absorbed. Remove from the heat and leave to rest for 10 minutes.

To make the pancakes, sift the flour and salt into a large bowl. Add the eggs and whisk until smooth. Slowly add the milk and water mixture, whisking all the time. You are aiming for a smooth batter with a single/light-cream consistency.

Melt the butter in a small frying pan over a low heat. Spoon 2 tablespoons of the melted butter into the batter and whisk it in. Pour the remaining butter into a bowl to use for cooking the pancakes.

Now increase the heat under the frying pan to medium. Spoon some of the batter into the frying pan and tilt the pan so that the batter covers the base. Cook for 1 minute on one side, lift the edge with a palette knife and flip over the pancake. Cook for a further 30 seconds on the other side. You want both sides to be golden and crispy. Slide the pancake onto a heatproof plate. Using the remaining butter and batter, make seven more pancakes and stack them onto the plate. Keep them warm in a low oven.

To finish the filling, put the chopped pecan nuts and sugar in a bowl and mix together. Put this pecan mix in a saucepan with the cream and cook over a medium heat, stirring, until it becomes the consistency of a thick purée. This will take about 8–10 minutes. Remove from the heat. Now add the cinnamon, sultanas/golden raisins, vanilla extract, lemon zest, jam and cooked red rice and mix well together.

Fill the pancakes with the pecan filling and roll or fold in quarters, then top with dollop of thick Greek yogurt.

Rice crispy waffles with orange & cardamom

Serves: 4
Prep: 10 minutes
Cook: 20 minutes

You will need a waffle-making machine for this. I'm sorry – I cannot abide recipes that require special culinary kit, especially when that kit is the stuff of fairgrounds and tacky market stalls. But cardamom, orange and rice crispies – such elegance scotched by such banality. This collision of flavours and textures is surreal and enough to warrant the gear. And once you have it, as I have found, you will use any excuse to pimp this waffle recipe with weird and wonderful flavour combinations ... morning, noon and night.

125g/4½oz/1 cup plain/
   all-purpose flour
40g/1½oz/⅓ cup wholemeal/
   whole-wheat flour
30g/1oz/heaped 1 cup rice
   crisp cereal
100g/3½oz/1 cup cornflour/
   cornstarch
90g/3¼oz/scant ½ cup soft
   brown sugar
1 tsp baking powder
½ tsp bicarbonate of soda/
   baking soda
¾ tsp salt
1 tsp freshly grated nutmeg
1 tbsp ground cardamom
1 tbsp grated orange zest
2 eggs, separated
350ml/12fl oz/1½ cups milk
120ml/4fl oz/½ cup corn oil
1 tsp vanilla extract
4 heaped tbsp plain yogurt
   or ice cream

Preheat your waffle iron. Mix together the dry ingredients in a large bowl.

Whisk the egg yolks, milk, oil and vanilla together in a separate bowl.

Whisk the egg whites in a large mixing bowl with a wire whisk or electric mixer until soft peaks form.

Mix the dry ingredients with the egg yolk mixture and stir until just combined. Gently fold in the egg whites.

Applying the mixture to the preheated iron, cook about 8 waffles in batches according the instructions for your waffle maker, keeping the cooked waffles warm in a low oven.

Top with a little fresh plain yogurt for breakfast or ice cream for a fairground-esque dessert.

Coconut rice spiced omelette

Serves: 4
Prep: 15 minutes
Cook: 45 minutes

This is great to make with leftover rice. It is dairy free, and the creamy coconut milk brings an exotic depth to this breakfast omelette. It is not uncommon for breakfast omelettes in the East to be bracing. Bracing is brought by chillies – fresh, green, fragrant and rousing. You can omit them entirely and just rely on the freshly snipped chives and coriander/cilantro to breathe a fresh green goodness into your morning. Serve with hunks of crusty bread, slathered in butter, if you like.

100g/3½oz/scant ½ cup white basmati rice, rinsed and drained
½ tbsp olive oil
2 small red onions, sliced
1 tsp ground coriander
¼ tsp ground cumin
1–3 green chillies, deseeded and finely chopped (optional – you choose your heat)
8 large eggs
120ml/4fl oz/½ cup coconut milk
1 tbsp desiccated/dried shredded coconut
1 tbsp finely snipped chives
1 tbsp chopped coriander/ cilantro leaves
1 tsp salt
freshly ground black pepper

Bring the rice and 240ml/8fl oz/1 cup water to the boil in a saucepan over a high heat. Reduce the heat to medium-low and simmer for about 10–15 minutes until all the water has been absorbed. Switch off the heat and cover with a tightly fitting lid. Leave in the pan to cool.

Preheat the oven to 180°C/350°F/Gas 4.

Heat the olive oil in a frying pan over a medium-high heat. Add the onions, ground coriander, cumin and green chillies and fry until the onions become translucent. Stir in the cooled rice and cook for about 3 minutes over a low heat until heated through.

Whisk the eggs, coconut milk, coconut, chives and coriander/cilantro leaves in a bowl. Season with the salt and pepper to taste. Pour the egg mixture into an ovenproof dish and distribute the rice mixture on top.

Cook in the oven for 20–25 minutes until set and golden.

Builder's breakfast bowl

Serves: 4
Prep: 10 minutes
Cook: 30 minutes

Leftover takeaway rice, university halls of residence, Sunday morning. Canned hot dog sausages instead of chorizo, canned tomatoes not fresh, and a knackered old enamel dish in lieu of the 'flameproof casserole'. There are a number of ways to skin a cat.

3 tbsp olive oil
100g/3½oz chorizo, sliced
200g/7oz cubed pancetta/
   diced bacon
8 mushrooms, sliced
4 tomatoes, peeled,
   deseeded and chopped
200g/7oz/heaped 1 cup
   risotto or other short-grain
   rice, rinsed and drained
55g/2oz canned cannellini
   beans, rinsed and drained
4 eggs
salt and freshly ground black
   pepper
tomato ketchup and brown
   sauce (optional)

Preheat the oven to 190°C/375°F/Gas 5.

Heat the oil in a shallow flameproof pan over a medium heat and fry the chorizo for a few minutes until the oil turns red and the aroma is smoky. Transfer the chorizo to a dish and leave to one side.

Add the pancetta to the pan and fry until slightly browned. Turn the heat up high and add the mushroom slices, then the tomatoes and cook on a high heat with the pancetta for 3–5 minutes until the mushrooms are soft.

Now turn the heat down to medium and add the rice. Stir-fry for 1 minute. Add enough water to cover – about 455ml/16fl oz/2 cups – and salt and pepper to taste. Bring to the boil, add the cannellini beans and return the chorizo to the pan. Cover with a tightly fitting lid and cook over a low heat for about 10–15 minutes until the rice is beginning to soften.

Break the eggs on top of the mixture, then put the pan in the oven, uncovered, and cook for 10 minutes until the eggs become firm and slightly browned.

For the full effect, serve warm with a shameless side dollop of good tomato ketchup ... and brown sauce if that's your thing.

Salmon blini sours

Serves: 4
Prep: 25 minutes, plus soaking and resting
Cook: 30 minutes

The Russian breakfast of choice, these have blini sophistication but a belly-filling base. The brown rice gives the blini base an earthy body that takes the robust, sour heat of the horseradish and sour cream topping. Go heavier with the lemon and horseradish if you want more of a wake-up call atop.

100g/3½oz/scant ½ cup long-grain brown rice, soaked for 2 hours, rinsed and drained
150g/5½oz/1 cup rice flour
¼ tsp salt
a pinch of cayenne pepper
1 tsp baking powder
2 eggs, separated
240ml/8fl oz/1 cup whole milk
olive oil, for greasing

THE SOUR CREAM TOPPING
85ml/2¾fl oz/⅓ cup sour cream or crème fraîche
½ tsp creamed horseradish
juice of ½ lemon
1 small red onion, finely diced
300g/10½oz smoked salmon
1 bunch of dill, small filaments pulled off
salt and freshly ground black pepper

Bring the rice and 240ml/8fl oz/1 cup water to the boil in a saucepan over a high heat. Reduce the heat to medium-low and simmer for about 10–15 minutes until all the water has been absorbed. Switch off the heat and cover with a tightly fitting lid. Leave the pan to cool.

Combine the cooked cooled brown rice with the flour, salt, cayenne and baking powder. Make a well in the middle.

Beat the egg yolks and milk together in a small bowl. Pour the milk and egg yolk mix into the rice mixture and stir well. Leave this to rest for 30 minutes.

Beat the egg whites until soft peaks form, then fold them into the rice batter.

Heat a frying pan over a medium heat. Brush lightly with oil. Now drop 1 tbsp of the batter onto the hot pan and gently encourage it into a circle using the back of a spoon. Your blinis should be about 4cm/1½in in diameter. Repeat the procedure to fill the frying pan.

Cook until bubbles appear on the top and the underside is golden, which takes about 3 minutes. Turn the blinis with a spatula and cook the other side for 2 minutes. Remove the cooked blinis from the heat and let them cool completely on a wire rack. Wipe the pan with a paper towel and lightly brush with more oil. Repeat until you have used all the batter. You should have about 16 blinis.

Mix together the sour cream, creamed horseradish, lemon juice and a small pinch of salt and pepper.

Top each cooled blini with a dollop of the sour cream topping, ½ tsp of diced red onion and a wave of smoked salmon. Use your artistry with the dill fronds to add a final bling to the blinis.

White basmati rice

A long-grain rice, white as snow with a hint of musk – this is the ultimate grain for Indians. I have to start here. I was brought up to see this grain as a minor god. Seriously. In India, you are cursed if you throw a single grain of rice away. I have enduring images of my mother rummaging through the bin after a dinner party, cussing and growling at the Philistine waste, scooping out the grains and putting them aside for her chickens.

More than that, culturally in the East, life is punctuated with rice ceremonies, like the first meal of a child in India, the 'Rice in the Mouth' celebration. Rice features as reverently as a priest at wedding ceremonies, religious ceremonies, even funeral ceremonies. I remember balls of rice being formed like matryoshka dolls at my father's funeral – each one representing one of his ancestors – in descending order of size.

I would be scolded senseless if I ever used the phrase 'we have run out of rice' in the home. Indians will never say this – they say 'we have too much rice'. To ensure some truth in this, whenever we take a cup of rice out of the grain store, we put three pinches back. Contrived and silly maybe, but luckily for us in our Western excess, we need not understand such desperation.

How to cook plain white rice

* Use 1 cup of rice to just under 2 cups of water (190g/6¾oz rice to 450ml/15fl oz water).

* Put the rice in a colander and rinse under cold running water until the water runs clear. Leave to drain.

* Put the rice in a saucepan and add the water. Bring to the boil, then simmer for about 10 minutes, uncovered, until almost dry with a dimpled surface.

* Cover tightly, remove from the heat and leave to stand for 15 minutes.

* Fluff up the grains with a fork.

Colonial kedgeree

Serves: 4
Prep: 20 minutes
Cook: 40 minutes

The origins of this dish are found in India in the days of the British Empire. *Kitchuri*, a simple rice and lentil stew, was found wanting by the British during the breakfasts of the Raj. Wanting, as it was a vegetarian lentil stew with neither hide nor hair of meat or fish. This would never do for a Brit's brunch. Indian chefs always bought fish first thing in the morning, and in the absence of refrigerators, that fish needed to be eaten before the height of the noon heat. This dish killed two birds with one stone. It stopped a redundant catch rotting in the heat. It also kept the memsahibs one piscatorial step removed from the brazen, heretical, lentil-worshipping vegetarianism that plagued the native kitchens.

2 tbsp ghee or clarified butter

¼ tsp cumin seeds

½ dried red chilli/hot pepper, leave in one piece

1 small bay leaf

5mm/¼in piece of fresh root ginger, peeled and grated

a pinch of chilli powder

½ tsp ground coriander

1 small onion, ½ chopped, ½ finely sliced

225g/8oz/heaped 1¼ cups white basmati rice, rinsed and drained

225g/8oz/1¼ cups brown lentils

½ tbsp turmeric

½ tsp salt

½ tbsp sunflower oil

½ tbsp flaked/slivered almonds

250g/9oz cooked smoked undyed haddock

2 hard-boiled eggs, shelled and quartered

a few sprigs of coriander/ cilantro

Melt the ghee in a large saucepan and add the cumin seeds. They need to pop and fizz. Add the dried red chilli and cook for a few seconds. Now add the bay leaf, ginger, chilli powder, ground coriander and chopped onion. Fry over a medium-low heat until the onion turns golden brown.

Add the rice, lentils, turmeric and salt and cook, stirring continuously, for 2 minutes.

Just cover with water, bring to the boil, then turn the heat down and simmer for 20–30 minutes until all the moisture has been absorbed and all the ingredients are tender, adding a little more boiling water, if necessary.

Meanwhile, heat the oil in a separate pan and fry the onion slivers until brown and crisp, then remove and drain well on paper towels. Brown the almonds quickly in the same pan.

Turn the kedgeree onto a large serving plate. Tear the cooked smoked haddock carefully into large chunky flakes and mix gently into the dish.

Scatter the fried onions and almonds on top. Wedge the quartered boiled eggs into the kedgeree and finally top with the coriander/cilantro sprigs.

Crumbled cloud crêpes

Serves: 4
Prep: 15 minutes
Cook: 25 minutes

I remember having something similar to this for breakfast in a Hungarian guest house. In Eastern Europe, they think nothing of making 40 crêpes in one go, piling them high on a plate and eating them over a couple of days. We need to lose our west-of-Budapest crêpe-phobia. Pancakes are not only for Tuesdays. Play with exciting, substantial toppings like this and they are splendid from Wednesday to Monday too. This pancake recipe uses rice flour. The rice flakes act as a gentle, sweet, creamy, cohesive force between the tang of the dairy and the pique of the chives.

THE GOATS' CHEESE FILLING

240ml/8fl oz/1 cup milk, plus
  extra if needed
¼ tsp caster/granulated
  sugar
55g/2oz/½ cup flaked rice
250g/9oz crumbly goats'
  cheese
1 tbsp thick plain yogurt
100ml/3½fl oz/scant ½ cup
  sour cream
1 large bunch of chives,
  chopped
salt and freshly ground black
  pepper

THE RICE FLOUR CRÊPES

150g/5½oz/1 cup rice flour
¼ tsp salt
2 eggs
240ml/8fl oz/1 cup whole
  milk
1 tbsp unsalted butter,
  melted
olive oil, for frying

To make the rice paste for the filling, put the milk, sugar and flaked rice in a saucepan and bring to the boil. Turn down the heat and simmer for 5 minutes.

Remove from the heat and leave to one side. Allow to cool and, as it does so, the rice will thicken. If you feel it has become too thick, feel free to loosen it with some extra milk. You are looking for a slightly thick, porridge-like consistency. Not concrete.

Put all the crêpe ingredients, except the frying oil, in a mixing bowl and whisk to a smooth pancake batter.

To make the filling, crumble the goats' cheese into a bowl and add the yogurt, sour cream, chives and the thickened rice paste mixture. Season with salt and pepper to taste and combine well.

The mixture will make about 8 large pancakes. To cook the pancakes, heat 1 teaspoon oil in a non-stick frying pan and swirl it around. Now add a ladleful of the pancake batter. Tilt the pan so that the batter covers the base of the pan and cook for 1 minute on each side. The pancake should be golden and crisp. Remove the pancake from the pan and repeat using the remaining batter, keeping the cooked pancakes warm in a low oven.

Spread some of the cheese and rice filling in a thin layer over each pancake. Roll up, or simply layer and serve.

Coconut rice hoppers

The name of this dish is *appam* – a sweet little word for a tender, porous, facecloth-soft, Keralan breakfast bread. This technique requires you to use a wok as it produces the perfect shallow bowl shape needed. The aim is for the batter to gather in the base of the pan making a thick, absorbent middle. This is usually a two-day preparation including fermentation time, but mine is a cheeky shortcut version, so expect some Indian-mother-in-law grief. In the South of India, these are served with sharp, resurrection-prompting curries. This is the perfect vehicle for your leftover korma, but I love them drizzled with maple syrup and a squeeze of lemon for breakfast – this puts *appam* on a very different map.

50g/1¾oz/heaped ¼ cup short-grain or long-grain white rice, rinsed and drained

2 tsp caster/granulated sugar

1 tsp dried yeast

½ tsp salt

240ml/8fl oz/1 cup coconut milk

150g/5½oz/1 cup rice flour

rapeseed/canola or soy oil, for frying

syrup, jam, leftover curry or ingredients of your choice, to serve

Put the rice in a small heavy-based pan with 240ml/8fl oz/1 cup water. Bring to the boil, then turn the heat down to low and simmer until the rice is tender, about 15 minutes. Remove the pan from the heat and drain the rice. Leave to one side and allow to cool.

Stir together the sugar and yeast with 4 tablespoons lukewarm water in a small mixing bowl. Leave this little brew to sit for 5 minutes.

Put the cooked rice, salt, coconut milk and 120ml/4fl oz/½ cup water in a bowl. Blend with a stick/immersion blender until it forms a very smooth batter.

Mix in the rice flour and 120ml/4fl oz/½ cup more water. Transfer this batter to a large lidded bowl and mix in the yeast mixture. Cover and leave in a warm place for 2 hours. Once the batter has doubled in volume, add a further 120ml/4fl oz/½ cup lukewarm water and stir gently.

Heat a small, lidded wok over a medium heat and brush the bottom and side with oil. Once the pan is hot, pour a ladleful of the batter into the pan and tilt the mixture around to coat the bottom the pan and make a little lip up the side of the pan. Cover the pan, reduce the heat to low and cook for 4–5 minutes until the edges of the *appam* begin to take on a light golden colour.

Remove the lid and cook for a further 30 seconds until the sides crisp a little more. Slide the *appam* onto a plate and keep warm in a low oven while you cook the remaining batter. You should end up with 8–10 *appam*, depending on the size of your pan.

Drizzle with syrup, jam, piquant leftover curry … it's not often these ingredients make the same sentence. Thank you, *appam*.

2

Light fantastics

Starters, lunches & late-night munchies

Serves: 4
Prep: 30 minutes
Cook: 1 hour
15 minutes

Cure-me-quick soup with chicken, noodles, ginger & lime

We all know chicken soup is dispensed in God's own pharmacy, but so often it tastes of dishwater. Not this one – it is full of big flavours that have big health benefits. The lime packs a good vitamin-C punch, the bones and skin perform their antibiotic magic, plus this big pan of golden goodness serves four, as I'm presuming you have infected your nearest and dearest. Look, freak not at the floating scum stage. Spoon a bit of it off but don't be too OCD. The mother soup will reabsorb any loose scum outriders and tame them into this goodness transfusion.

1 tbsp olive oil

2 chicken breasts, skin on

2 chicken thighs, skin on

1 small onion, diced

2 garlic cloves, crushed

240ml/8fl oz/1 cup white wine

grated zest and juice of 2 limes

5cm/2in piece of fresh root ginger, peeled and halved

4 whole black peppercorns

2 chicken stock cubes, crumbled

2 bay leaves

2 tsp caster/granulated sugar

2 carrots, peeled and sliced

2 celery stalks, diced

1 tbsp finely chopped thyme leaves

115g/4oz fine rice noodles

salt and freshly ground black pepper

a few coriander/cilantro sprigs

Heat the olive oil in a large saucepan over a medium heat, add the chicken, onion, and crushed garlic cloves and cook for about 5 minutes until the chicken breast is browned and the onions start to turn translucent.

Now pour the wine, lime juice and 1 litre/35fl oz/4⅓ cups water over the chicken mixture. Slice one half of the ginger and add it to the pan with the peppercorns, chicken stock cubes, bay leaves and sugar. Bring to the boil, then turn the heat down to medium-low and simmer for 45 minutes.

Remove the chicken pieces from the soup to a cutting board. Shred the breast and thighs into small pieces, discarding the bones and skin.

Add the carrots, celery, half the lime zest and the thyme to the soup. Reduce the heat to low and cook until the vegetables begin to soften, about 20 minutes.

Bring the soup to the boil. Return the chicken to the soup along with the noodles. Mince the remaining ginger and add it to the pan. Remove the pan from heat, cover and leave to one side until the noodles have softened. This should take about 10 minutes.

Season with salt and pepper to taste, then top with the coriander/cilantro and the remaining lime zest to serve.

Red rice

Widely available, this is a short-grained, unmilled rice with a deep red outer colour, giving way to a pale centre. It has more texture and bite than white rice and takes longer to cook. It retains its colour when cooked and makes a nutrient-full, chewier, fun alternative to brown or white rice. The most common is the Camargue red rice of the wetlands of southern France, but you can also enjoy Thai red rice – both are sticky and full of deep flavours – or Bhutanese red rice, a medium grain borne out of the kingdom of Bhutan, cultivated in the shadow of the Himalayas. It has an earthy flavour and turns pink on cooking. Slightly sticky, it can be used instead of brown rice to give a russet splendour to any dish.

I hate to keep harping on about my youth, but I do remember bringing a bag of this stuff into my mother's kitchen and realizing it would have been more acceptable to have turned up blind drunk with a tattoo. 'It smells of mollychop' (the stuff we fed the pony). 'It has no elegance – you have no elegance. It's brash,' she berated me. 'What the hell is wrong with you?' she went on. But, blimey, I loved it.

I never knew rice could have so much to say. It will bellow over a more subtle dish, so it needs to be paired with deep, rich dishes that hold their own, for instance, my Hungarian Cherry Red Soup (see opposite). It is stunning to look at – I love its subversive and brassy hue, the antithesis of its emasculated white cousin. It's also so easy to cook, less precious and eager to please. Invest in it and make forever brazen a corner of your kitchen.

How to cook red rice

The French use the straining method and I advise that with this nutty, knobbly grain.

* Use 1 cup of rice to 2 cups of water (190g/6¾oz rice to 480ml/16fl oz water).

* Put the rice and water in a saucepan, bring to the boil, then simmer gently for about 30 minutes, uncovered, until you have a soft finish but still with a little bite.

* Strain, if necessary, then fluff up the grains with a fork.

However, the absorption method (see page 12) works very well too, simmering for 25 minutes, then leaving the grain to stand for 20 minutes.

Cherry red soup

Serves: 4
Prep: 10 minutes, plus standing and chilling
Cook: 1 hour

Hungarian dishes care not for our conservative boundaries of propriety. They often trigger dissonance in the minds of Western foodies. This is based on the Hungarian cold cherry soup, *megyleves*. Cold ... cherry ... and ... soup. This sentence makes no sense. I recall it sounding like nails down my culinary blackboard. But I ate this soup on the banks of the Danube in Budapest on a scorching day. It opened my mind. It was movingly refreshing, elegant and full of texture. By Jove, I thought, I have so much to learn.

100g/3½oz/heaped ½ cup red rice, rinsed and drained

700g/1lb 9oz fresh morello or sour cherries, washed and pitted, or canned cherries and their juice

a pinch of ground cinnamon

a pinch of freshly grated nutmeg

grated zest and juice of 1 lemon

75g/2½oz/heaped ⅓ cup caster/granulated sugar

1 large egg yolk

250ml/8fl oz/1 cup sour cream

6 small mint leaves

2 tbsp chopped pistachios

Put the rice in a heavy-based saucepan with 300ml/10½fl oz/generous 1¼ cups water. Bring to the boil over a medium-high heat, then turn the heat down to low and simmer for about 30 minutes, uncovered, until the grains are soft. Switch off the heat, cover, and leave the pan to stand for 10 minutes. Strain and leave to one side.

Reserve a few whole cherries to finish the dish - either fresh or canned. Put the remaining fruit in a large saucepan. Add the spices, lemon zest and juice. Cover with 240ml/8fl oz/1 cup water and add the sugar. Bring to the boil, then simmer over a medium-low heat for 10 minutes. Remove half the cherries using a slotted spoon and put them in a blender. Blitz until you have a smooth purée. Return this blend to the soup and return the soup to the boil.

Now mix the egg yolk and sour cream in a bowl. Add a cup of the cherry soup and stir to mix well. Return the mixture to the rest of the soup. Simmer very gently for around 3 minutes, then remove from the heat and stir in the cooled red rice mixture. Sprinkle with the mint and pistachios, add the reserved cherries and chill until ready to serve.

Lemony egg soup

Serves: 4
Prep: 10 minutes
Cook: 15 minutes

I was lucky enough to have a good Cypriot pal with a mother who cooked like a fiend. She called this *avgolemono* soup – what a weird word, I thought, at the age of ten – but not nearly as funny as the ingredients. I resolved to hate it ... but it was divine.

900ml/31fl oz/3¾ cups good chicken stock
55g/2oz/scant ⅓ cup long-grain white rice, rinsed and drained
3 egg yolks
2–3 tbsp lemon juice
2 tbsp finely chopped parsley leaves
salt and freshly ground black pepper

Bring the stock to the boil in a saucepan and add the rice. Simmer for 12 minutes over a medium heat until the rice is just soft. Remove from the heat and season with salt and pepper.

Whisk the egg yolks, add 2 tablespoons of the lemon juice and continue to whisk until the mixture is smooth and frothy.

Add a cup full of soup to the egg mix and whisk again. Now slowly add the egg mix to the soup, whisking all the time. Season with salt and 1 teaspoon pepper and add more lemon juice if you fancy a slightly tarter soup.

Spoon into bowls and serve sprinkled with the chopped parsley. The fresh green is beautiful against the sunshine yellow of this soup.

Serves: 4
Prep: 10 minutes
Cook: 15 minutes

Goodness! green soup with rice & watercress

This is a great way to bring heaps of goodly greens into your diet in the form of a quick, simple and hearty soup. Take your pick of greens. I love using a watercress and kale combo.

80g/2¾oz/scant ½ cup white basmati rice, rinsed and drained

2 tbsp olive oil

1 large onion, diced

2 garlic cloves, finely chopped

¼ tsp white pepper

¼ tsp freshly grated nutmeg

1 litre/35fl oz/4⅓ cups chicken or vegetable stock

150g/5½oz green leaves of your choice, such as spinach, kale, sorrel, watercress or rocket/arugula

1 handful of coriander/cilantro leaves

½ tsp ground cumin

1 tbsp caster/granulated sugar

juice of ½ lemon

salt and freshly ground black pepper

4 tbsp sour cream or crème fraîche, to swirl in at the end

crusty bread

In a heavy-based pan, bring 1 litre/35fl oz/4⅓ cups water to the boil over a high heat and add the rice. Return to the boil, then turn the heat down to medium and simmer brightly for about 8 minutes until the rice is almost tender. Drain and rinse with cold water to stop the cooking process.

Heat the oil in a deep pan and fry the onion and garlic over a medium-low heat until the onion becomes translucent. Add the pepper, nutmeg and stock. Add the rice, bring to the boil, then simmer over a medium-low heat for 10 minutes.

Carefully lower the greens into the pan with the coriander/cilantro, cumin, sugar and lemon juice, then simmer for a further 4 minutes. Season generously with salt and pepper.

Now the simple drama. Remove the pan from the heat and plunge in a stick/immersion blender. Pulse until you have a thick, smooth consistency.

Pour into bowls and swirl with sour cream or add a dollop of crème fraîche. Serve immediately with thick crusty bread.

Hot soy hen noodles

Serves: 4
Prep: 10 minutes
Cook: 1 hour

I remember the first time I tried Hainanese chicken and rice, and being sceptical that something so anaemic-looking could carry any flavour weight. On tasting it, I recall my shame in doubting ancient Chinese alchemists and their ability to draw flavour out of anodyne chicken, charming it to dance with ginger in an amazing Hainanese tarantella. This dish is my noodle nod to that thrill.

1.2kg/2lb 12oz whole chicken

2 spring onions/scallions, cut into 5cm/2in lengths

5 sprigs of coriander/cilantro, plus extra leaves, to serve

¾ tsp salt

2.5cm/1in piece of fresh root ginger, peeled and roughly smashed

½ tsp whole black peppercorns

250g/9oz flat rice noodles

2 tbsp light soy sauce

1 tbsp toasted sesame oil

1–2 red chillies, deseeded and diced

THE HAINANESE SAUCE

3 tbsp sunflower oil

2 spring onions/scallions, sliced

1 tbsp finely grated fresh root ginger

1 tsp salt

4–5 tbsp light soy sauce

Rinse the chicken, drain and remove any fat from the cavity opening and around the neck. Cut off the parson's nose and discard it, unless you come from a culture that reveres them.

Put the chicken in a large clay pot or casserole dish and add the spring onions/scallions, coriander/cilantro, salt, ginger, peppercorns and enough water to cover the chicken. Cover and bring to the boil, then turn the heat down to low and simmer very gently for 35 minutes. Turn off the heat and leave the chicken for 10 minutes until the juices run clear when you pierce the thigh with a knife.

Remove the chicken from the pot and drain well. Skim off any scum from the stock and scoop out the floating ingredient detritus.

Now put the pot back on the stove and bring the stock back to the boil. Switch off the heat and plunge in the rice noodles. Stir every so often. You are waiting for them to become limp and soft but with some bite remaining. This should take around 10 minutes. Once they are ready, remove them from the stock and drain them.

Put the noodles in a large bowl and toss with the soy sauce and sesame oil. Leave to one side.

To make the sauce, heat a wok over a high heat, add the oil and heat until it just begins to smoke. Now add the spring onions/scallions, ginger, salt and light soy sauce and stir well. Cook for 30 seconds, then quickly toss in the soft rice noodles and stir until they are completely covered with the sauce. Lift them out of the pan and transfer to a large serving plate, leaving some sauce in the wok.

Put the whole chicken on top of the noodles and pour over the light soy dressing, scatter with the sliced red chillies and coriander/cilantro leaves. Serve with pronged fork and carving knife to pull the soft chicken apart into portions.

Serves: 4
Prep: 10 minutes
Cook: 20 minutes

Rice crispy rubble chicken with cumin, thyme & paprika

Chicken, dipped in pimped mayonnaise and spiced breakfast cereal, is finding its way into many a kitchen across the globe, but it's a guilty pleasure. Not a recipe you would put into words and admit to. I added the words 'cumin', 'thyme' and 'paprika' in an attempt, not just to give this shameless act of poultry rubbling a veneer of grace, but because they make these knobbly, garish goujons utterly delicious.

100g/3½oz/3 cups crispy
   rice cereal
½ tsp paprika
½ tsp ground cumin
½ tsp dried thyme
a pinch of salt
1 garlic clove, crushed
a squeeze of lemon juice
200ml/7fl oz/scant 1 cup
   mayonnaise
4 skinless, boneless chicken
   breasts, cut into thick strips
tomato ketchup

Preheat the oven to 200°C/400°F/Gas 6 and line a shallow baking sheet with baking parchment.

Put the cereal in a food bag and crush roughly. Now add the paprika, cumin, thyme and salt and mix well. Pour onto a plate.

Mix together the garlic, lemon juice and mayonnaise in a separate bowl.

Coat the chicken strips in a thin layer of the mayonnaise mix. Toss them in the cereal mix and put on the baking sheet one at a time. Bake for 15–20 minutes until golden, turning half way through cooking.

Serve with a dollop of tomato ketchup, recklessness and napkins – and don't even attempt any healthy side-dish token gestures. Enjoy!

Japanese egg rice rolls

For Japanese children, this is beans on toast. It's a great use for leftover fried or plain rice, but if you do need to cook the rice first, you'll need two-thirds of a cup of raw rice. The rolls barefacedly use tomato ketchup as a lube. They are ready in no time and eaten with the hands – an after-school no-brainer.

115ml/3¾fl oz/scant ½ cup
   vegetable or soy oil
1 small onion, chopped
½ carrot, peeled and diced
1 skinless, boneless chicken
   thigh, diced
2 mushrooms, finely diced
 – great if you can find
   shiitake but not necessary
1 tbsp chopped coriander/
   cilantro leaves
270g/9½oz/2 cups cooked
   long-grain white rice
2 tbsp tomato ketchup, plus
   extra to serve
6 eggs, lightly beaten
4 tbsp whole or soy milk
salt and freshly ground black
   pepper

Heat 4 tablespoons of the oil in a frying pan and add the onion. Once translucent, add the carrot and the chicken and cook until the meat is slightly browned.

Add the mushrooms and stir-fry over a medium-high heat until they soften. Season with salt and pepper and remove the mixture from the pan. Once slightly cooled, stir in the chopped coriander/cilantro.

Heat 2 tablespoons of the oil in the pan and add the cold cooked rice. Once it is heated through, add the meat and vegetable mixture, then the tomato ketchup and season with salt and pepper to taste. Simple. Put this mixture to one side.

Beat the eggs and milk together in a bowl. You are going to make a plain, thin omelette with this mixture.

Pour a little of the remaining oil into an wide-based frying pan. Once hot, pour in a quarter of the egg mixture and allow it to set for 1 minute. Keep the heat on low and spoon a quarter of the rice mixture over one half. Fold the omelette over the rice mixture and after a minute more on low heat, slide the folded, filled egg roll onto a plate. Repeat with the remaining rolls. Serve as a finger snack with more tomato ketchup.

Sticky or glutinous rice

A bit of science but a pretty tale, I think. Geneticists say that a thousand years ago, somewhere deep in South East Asia, a lowly farmer stumbled upon a freak rice plant with a grain that was stickier than normal. This adventurous soul boiled it up and found enlightenment in this single genetic mutation. Sticky rice is now the staple food in many areas in South East Asia, China and Japan.

Normal rice has two starches: amylose and amylopectin. Sticky rice lacks amylose and this makes it sticky. This has been traced back to a single evolutionary origin. How uniquely wonderful that this one plant, a deficient anomaly of nature, found a farming family that loved it enough to make it the standard bearer for rice across the globe.

Different nations claim glutinous rice as their own. The Chinese call theirs *geng* rice and this is the favoured rice for dim sum and sweet rice dishes – it has a black and a white form. Japanese glutinous rice is sweet – and this for the Japanese is no bad thing. The Thai glutinous rice also comes in black and white forms. The black rice cooks to a dramatic purple, which sits well with the intense flavours of some of the Thai rice-based desserts.

How to cook plain sticky rice

This tough-coated grain does need a good soak to ensure stickiness. You can either steam or boil the rice.

* Soak the rice in cold water for at least an hour, or overnight, then drain.

To steam:
* To steam: line a steamer with muslin/cheesecloth and pour in the rice. Cover with the lid and steam over a medium-high heat for about 30 minutes until tender.

To boil:
* Use 1 cup of rice to just under 2 cups of water (190g/6¾oz rice to 450ml/15fl oz water).

* Put the rice in a colander and rinse under cold running water until the water runs clear. Leave to drain.

* Put the rice and water in a saucepan, bring to the boil, then simmer for 15 minutes, partially covered, until almost dry with a dimpled surface.

* Cover tightly, remove from the heat and leave to stand for 20 minutes.

Lotus leaf parcels

Serves: 4
Prep: 30 minutes, plus soaking
Cook: 1 hour 25 minutes

I love the anxious, greedy unwrapping of these virgin parcels of Chinese wizardry. There are so many ways the flavours could have blended within – what flavour combinations might each one hold? Lotus leaves, there is no getting around. They are not just a dull wrapper, they bring so much flavour to the party. You can easily buy them in Asian supermarkets and online.

300g/10½oz/heaped 1½ cups sticky rice
2 large lotus leaves

THE CHINESE FILLING
1 tbsp dried shrimp
2 dried Chinese mushrooms
1 tbsp sunflower oil
100g/3½oz skinless, boneless chicken breast, finely diced
1 small garlic clove, crushed
1 spring onion/scallion, chopped
1 Chinese sausage (lap cheong), thinly sliced
½ tbsp oyster sauce
½ tbsp light soy sauce
½ tbsp sugar
½ tsp toasted sesame oil
½ tbsp cornflour/cornstarch
chilli sauce

Cover the rice with water the night before you want to cook this dish and leave to soak. Wash and drain the rice three times, then put in a bamboo steamer lined with muslin/cheesecloth. Steam for 30–40 minutes. When the rice is cooked, leave to cool slightly.

Meanwhile, soak the dried shrimp in boiling water for 45 minutes and the dried mushrooms in boiling water for 30 minutes. When soft, drain the mushrooms and squeeze out any excess water. Drain the shrimp.

Submerge the lotus leaves in boiled water for 10 minutes. They need to be soft. Shake them dry and cut them to give four equal pieces.

Start making the filling by heating a wok to a high heat, add half the oil and stir-fry the chicken until browned. Add the shrimp, mushrooms, garlic, spring onion/scallion and sausage and continue to fry for 2 minutes.

Add the oyster sauce, soy sauce, sugar and sesame oil and toss well. Mix the cornflour/cornstarch with 200ml/7fl oz/scant 1 cup water and add to the sauce. Simmer, stirring, until the sauce thickens.

Divide the cooled rice into 8 balls, wetting your hands first to stop it sticking to you.

Put the lotus leaf pieces on a flat surface, shiny-side up, vein-side down. Put a rice ball on one leaf, flatten it slightly and make an indentation in the middle. Spoon a quarter of the filling into the indentation, flatten a second rice ball and gently put it on top, then smooth the rice into one ball. Wrap the ball up firmly by folding the leaves over to form an envelope. Repeat to make three more parcels.

Set up a steaming rack in a wok of boiling water, add the parcels, cover and steam for 30 minutes.

To serve, open up each parcel and serve the rice pocket in its housing leaf. Enjoy hot with chilli sauce on the side.

Nasi goreng

Serves: 4
Prep: 20 minutes
Cook: 30 minutes

It was the San Franciscan street-vendor version of this Indonesian classic that snagged on my rice DNA. I love the twisted luxury of a crisp fried egg oozing rich salted yolk into the sweet tangy rice. The key is the kecap manis (Indonesian sweet soy sauce). Invest in some and – whether you have a few cups of leftover rice or you cook from scratch – you'll be minutes away from a classic pimped rice dish.

140g/5oz/scant ¾ cup basmati rice, rinsed and drained

125g/4½oz green beans, trimmed and cut into bite-size lengths

2 large shallots, finely sliced

5 tbsp sunflower oil, plus extra for frying

2 skinless, boneless chicken breasts, cut into thin strips

170g/6oz raw prawns/shrimp, shelled and de-veined

1 tbsp kecap manis

6 spring onions/scallions, finely sliced

1 large handful of coriander/cilantro leaves, finely chopped, plus extra to serve

4 eggs

salt

chilli oil

THE SHRIMP & CHILLI PASTE

100g/3½oz dried shrimp

2 garlic cloves

3 large red chillies or bird's eye chillies, deseeded amd chopped

3 tbsp roasted peanuts, chopped

Put the rice in a saucepan with 350ml/12fl oz/1½ cups water. Bring to the boil, then simmer for 10 minutes, uncovered, until almost dry. Cover tightly, remove from the heat and leave for 15 minutes. Alternatively, use 400g/14oz/3 cups cooked rice.

Soak the dried shrimp for the paste in 240ml/8fl oz/1 cup water for 10 minutes, then drain, reserving the soaking liquid.

Cook the green beans in boiling water for 1 minute, then drain and leave to one side.

Fry the shallots in 3 tablespoons of the sunflower oil over a medium heat. You are going to want them brown, crisp and sweet, so fry them in small batches and remove them as you go – you don't want a melted white sludge. As soon as each batch is brown, drain them on paper towels and leave to one side to cool.

Make the paste by blending the drained shrimps with all the other paste ingredients in a food processor until coarsely chopped. Add just enough of the reserved water from the soaked shrimp to loosen the paste a little.

Heat the remaining oil in a large wok over a medium-high heat. Add the paste and fry briskly for a couple of minutes. Add the chicken and fry until just lightly browned, then add the cooked beans. They will need to fry until they are cooked through. We are now in the end stages of the dish.

Next, add the prawns/shrimp, tossing them in the hot sauce until they turn pink. Turn the heat down to low and add the rice. The paste and sauce will quietly infuse into the soft grain. Add the kecap manis – this is the tangy sweet heart and soul of a good nasi goreng – and season with salt. If at any point you want to make the dish more moist, add a little more shrimp water. Toss in the spring onions/scallions and coriander/cilantro.

Meanwhile, fry the eggs in hot oil sunny-side up, bottom brown and gnarled. To serve, divide the rice mix equally among serving bowls and put a fried egg on top. Sprinkle with a little coriander/cilantro and the crispy shallots and serve with chilli oil for guests to add to taste.

Inca salad

Serves: 4
Prep: 30 minutes
Cook: 40 minutes

Although Peruvian in origin, there is something *Abigail's Party*-tastic about this salad – particularly if you serve it in a glass salad dish and layer it like Zippy's rainbow. I like to drag it from the seventies to a present, rough-hewn chic by piling it rustically on a big wooden platter and letting the gorgeous kaleidoscope tumble where it will.

115g/4oz/scant ⅔ cup long-grain brown rice, soaked for 2 hours, rinsed and drained

1 red pepper, deseeded and halved

1 small onion, sliced

olive oil, for drizzling

1 tbsp chopped coriander/ cilantro leaves

115g/4oz fresh green beans, halved

50g/1¾oz baby sweetcorn

1 avocado

juice of ½ lemon

75g/2½oz mixed salad leaves

100g/3½oz cooked ham, chopped

1 tbsp capers, rinsed and drained

10 pepper-stuffed olives, halved

4 hard-boiled eggs, quartered

THE YOGURT DRESSING

1 garlic clove, crushed

½ tsp granulated sugar

½ tsp wholegrain mustard

3 tbsp plain yogurt

2 tbsp lemon juice

3 tbsp sunflower oil

4 tbsp olive oil

salt and freshly ground black pepper

Put the rice and 500ml/16fl oz/2 cups water in a heavy-based pan and bring to the boil over a medium-high heat. Turn the heat down to medium-low and simmer for 10 minutes until almost all the water has been absorbed. Clamp on a tight lid, remove from the heat and leave the pan for 10 minutes. Allow the rice to cool.

Preheat the grill/broiler. Put the halved pepper and the onion on a small baking sheet and drizzle with a little olive oil. Grill/broil until the pepper becomes blackened and blistered and the onion turns golden brown. Turn the peppers and mix the onions a little so they are evenly cooked. Leave to one side to cool.

Once cooled, remove the skin from the peppers and cut into strips.

Prepare the yogurt dressing by placing all the ingredients in a bowl and whisking until smooth. Season with salt and pepper.

Put the cooked rice into a large salad bowl and mix with half the dressing and half the chopped coriander/cilantro. Stir the grilled/broiled onions into the rice mix.

Half-fill a heavy-based saucepan with water and bring it to the boil. Add the green beans and cook for 2 minutes. Now add the sweetcorn and cook for a couple of minutes until tender. Drain the vegetables and run them under a cold tap to stop the cooking process.

While they are cooking, peel, pit and slice the avocado and toss in a little of the lemon juice.

Mix the avocado with the salad leaves, beans, sweetcorn, ham and red pepper strips. Add the remaining salad dressing, a squeeze of lemon juice and a pinch of salt and toss carefully.

Now spoon the salad mixture over the rice. Scatter the capers, olives and remaining coriander/cilantro on top and tuck the boiled-egg quarters in amongst the dressed vegetables.

Pleasant peasant omelette

Although it uses straightforward, country ingredients, there really is nothing peasant-like in the royal combination of smoke-rich chorizo and graceful rice grains. Canned chickpeas are ever-ready, generous little flavour-mules, adding substance and texture to this simple, hearty supper.

2 tomatoes

3 tbsp sunflower oil

1 onion, chopped

200g/7oz chorizo, sliced

175g/6oz skinless, boneless chicken breasts, diced

350g/12oz/scant 2 cups risotto rice, rinsed and drained

1 litre/35fl oz/4⅓ cups chicken stock

115g/4oz/heaped ¾ cup cooked or canned chickpeas

6 eggs

juice of ½ orange

1 tsp chopped parsley leaves

salt and freshly ground black pepper

Score a cross on the top of each tomato, then plunge into a bowl of boiling water, then a bowl of cold water. Leave until cool enough to handle, then peel off the skin and chop the flesh.

Preheat the oven to 190°C/375°F/Gas 5 and select a lidded, flameproof casserole dish.

Heat the oil in the casserole, add the onion and chorizo and fry over a medium heat until golden. Add the tomatoes and fry for a few minutes. Add the chicken and fry until browned.

Add the rice and stir for about a minute, then pour in the stock and season with salt and pepper to taste. Bring to the boil, then turn the heat down to low. Add the chickpeas, cover the dish tightly with a lid and cook on the hob for 15 minutes on a low heat until the rice is tender and all the liquid has been absorbed. Remove the pan from the heat.

Beat together the eggs and orange juice. Pour this mixture over the rice and put the casserole in the oven, uncovered, for 10 minutes until the eggs have become slightly brown. Sprinkle with a little chopped parsley and serve hot.

Quick porky cashew pot

There is nothing grand about this dish. As a vehicle for your leftover rice, those waning grains, forgotten and brittle, become soft and resurrected in the glow of soy and pork. Basic cuts from your freezer stash and an ignominious bag of cashews from the petrol station, *et voila* – a shamelessly piggy supper for four. Of course, if you don't have any leftover rice, just cook ⅔ cup rice following the method on page 42.

2 tbsp sunflower oil

2 onions, diced

2.5cm/1in piece of fresh root ginger, peeled and grated

2 garlic cloves, chopped

85g/3oz/scant ¾ cup cashew nuts (a bag of roasted salted nuts would do)

2 carrots, peeled and diced

2 tbsp soft brown sugar

225g/8oz pork loin, diced

2 tsp salt

3 tbsp light soy sauce

270g/9½oz/2 cups cooked long-grain white or brown rice

1 tbsp chopped coriander/ cilantro leaves

chilli oil (optional)

Heat the oil in a frying pan over a medium heat, add the onions, ginger and garlic and fry until they are good and brown. Throw in the cashew nuts and toss them in the mixture for about 2 minutes.

Add the carrots and brown sugar and fry for about 5 minutes until the carrots have softened. Add the pork and cook on a brisk heat until the meat is beginning to brown. Add the salt and soy sauce, loosen the dish with 120ml/4fl oz/½ cup water and allow to bubble through.

Toss in the cooked rice and once it has heated through, transfer to a serving dish and sprinkle with the chopped coriander/cilantro. Serve hot with chilli oil for guests to add to taste, if they wish.

Inca salad

Serves: 4
Prep: 30 minutes
Cook: 40 minutes

Although Peruvian in origin, there is something *Abigail's Party*-tastic about this salad – particularly if you serve it in a glass salad dish and layer it like Zippy's rainbow. I like to drag it from the seventies to a present, rough-hewn chic by piling it rustically on a big wooden platter and letting the gorgeous kaleidoscope tumble where it will.

115g/4oz/scant ⅔ cup long-grain brown rice, soaked for 2 hours, rinsed and drained

1 red pepper, deseeded and halved

1 small onion, sliced

olive oil, for drizzling

1 tbsp chopped coriander/cilantro leaves

115g/4oz fresh green beans, halved

50g/1¾oz baby sweetcorn

1 avocado

juice of ½ lemon

75g/2½oz mixed salad leaves

100g/3½oz cooked ham, chopped

1 tbsp capers, rinsed and drained

10 pepper-stuffed olives, halved

4 hard-boiled eggs, quartered

THE YOGURT DRESSING

1 garlic clove, crushed

½ tsp granulated sugar

½ tsp wholegrain mustard

3 tbsp plain yogurt

2 tbsp lemon juice

3 tbsp sunflower oil

4 tbsp olive oil

salt and freshly ground black pepper

Put the rice and 500ml/16fl oz/2 cups water in a heavy-based pan and bring to the boil over a medium-high heat. Turn the heat down to medium-low and simmer for 10 minutes until almost all the water has been absorbed. Clamp on a tight lid, remove from the heat and leave the pan for 10 minutes. Allow the rice to cool.

Preheat the grill/broiler. Put the halved pepper and the onion on a small baking sheet and drizzle with a little olive oil. Grill/broil until the pepper becomes blackened and blistered and the onion turns golden brown. Turn the peppers and mix the onions a little so they are evenly cooked. Leave to one side to cool.

Once cooled, remove the skin from the peppers and cut into strips.

Prepare the yogurt dressing by placing all the ingredients in a bowl and whisking until smooth. Season with salt and pepper.

Put the cooked rice into a large salad bowl and mix with half the dressing and half the chopped coriander/cilantro. Stir the grilled/broiled onions into the rice mix.

Half-fill a heavy-based saucepan with water and bring it to the boil. Add the green beans and cook for 2 minutes. Now add the sweetcorn and cook for a couple of minutes until tender. Drain the vegetables and run them under a cold tap to stop the cooking process.

While they are cooking, peel, pit and slice the avocado and toss in a little of the lemon juice.

Mix the avocado with the salad leaves, beans, sweetcorn, ham and red pepper strips. Add the remaining salad dressing, a squeeze of lemon juice and a pinch of salt and toss carefully.

Now spoon the salad mixture over the rice. Scatter the capers, olives and remaining coriander/cilantro on top and tuck the boiled-egg quarters in amongst the dressed vegetables.

At the heart of the cuisine

Rice was introduced to South and Central America and the Caribbean by the Spanish when they colonized the region in the 1520s, bringing Asian rice to Mexico and other far-flung shores. It is said that the African slaves, transported by the Portuguese, also had an influential role in the establishment of rice as a firm South American staple. The dish of rice and peas was an obvious vehicle for rice and from there, the South American countries took the grain and danced it into the heart of their cuisine, where it remains firmly ensconced. Many nations have their own unique way of cooking rice and demand different textures and different colours from their rice dishes.

Nicaragua is known for serving rice and peas at every single meal. This they call *gallo pinto*, and it is a huge Costa Rican favourite, too. As in Britain, where everyone knows how to make a good pot of tea, in Costa Rica, everyone has a *gallo pinto* recipe in their deft fingers.

Ecuadorians prefer to serve their main dishes with *arros amarillo*, or yellow rice, as a side dish. The yellow colour comes from *annatto* or *achiote*, a natural food dye. Due to the high altitudes in Ecuador, rice needs to cook for longer than at lower levels, so the skill of a really good Ecuadorian chef involves getting a perfect nutty finish, not a soft, over-boiled, altitude-sickness-inducing mass.

Peruvians create a stunning white rice dish that is simply eaten on its own, and is known as *arroz graneado*, which translates as 'grained rice'. It is essentially a rice dish that is started off with oil and garlic, then the rice is cooked in stock. Cooking rice in this way adds a huge amount of punch and flavour.

Pearly pork urchins

Serves: 4
Prep: 20 minutes, plus soaking
Cook: 40 minutes

This simple Chinese dish always reminds me of little sea urchins. They provide a fun obstacle course for the tongue. The sticky rice grains coating the meat balls become pearly in the cooking process and stand to an enticing attention. Like the pearl, however, sticky rice needs time to develop so give it a good overnight soak before you make this dish if you can.

325g/11½oz/1¾ cups sticky rice
450g/1lb minced/ground pork
1 large spring onion/scallion, finely chopped
70g/2½oz water chestnuts, finely chopped
1 egg white
1½ tbsp finely chopped fresh root ginger
2 tbsp light soy sauce
1 tbsp Shaoxing rice wine
1 tsp salt
1 tbsp cornflour/cornstarch
1½ tsp toasted sesame oil
dark soy sauce, for dipping

Soak the rice overnight. Just before you start cooking, drain it well and spread the grains out on a baking sheet.

Combine all the remaining ingredients except the sesame oil and dark soy sauce. Roll the mixture into 24 x 2cm/¾in balls and then roll each meatball in the rice so that it is coated. Put the balls on a heatproof plate about 1cm/½in apart. You will need to do a few at a time.

Put the plate in a steamer and cook in batches. They will need to steam for around 20 minutes until they are cooked through. You are waiting for the rice to soften and for the pork to cook through. When cooked, drizzle with the sesame oil.

Serve hot with the soy dipping sauce.

Parma ham & pea risotto

Risottos are such a comforting duvet of carbs, they need the odd subversive twist to keep the palate awake. Parmesan is the usual culprit, a sweetly pungent, smooth operator. Parma ham is another great wake-up call – a salty bacon slam dunker. I love a squeeze of lemon at the end just to give that final citrus jolt, but I know the very thought of this would cause many an Italian mamma a culinary hernia. This particular risotto makes a great light meal, or you can serve it with white fish or poultry dishes.

2 tbsp olive oil

1 onion, finely chopped

400g/14oz/scant 2¼ cups risotto rice, rinsed and drained

120ml/4fl oz/½ cup dry white wine

900ml/31fl oz/generous 3¾ cups hot chicken stock

55g/2oz/½ cup frozen peas

75g/3oz Parma ham/ prosciutto, cut into strips

30g/1oz/2 tbsp butter

30g/1oz/scant ½ cup freshly grated Parmesan cheese

salt and freshly ground black pepper

1–2 lemons, cut into wedges

Heat the oil in a heavy-based saucepan and fry the onion until translucent. Stir in the rice and cook for 2 minutes, stirring constantly. Add the wine and continue to stir until the wine has been absorbed.

Now begin to add the stock a ladleful at a time, waiting for each ladle to be absorbed before you add the next. This will take about 20 minutes. Once the rice is nearly cooked, add the peas and Parma ham/prosciutto and cook until the risotto is creamy.

Stir in the butter and Parmesan and season with salt and pepper to taste. Serve warm with the suggestive lemon wedges on the side.

Transylvanian meatloaf

Serves: 4–6
Prep: 30 minutes
Cook: 1 hour

Meatloaf, on a menu, I find irresistible. It never pretends to be a light option. It is what it says on the tin but better. It has hidden patterns and secret ingredients that only reveal themselves once you commit and slice through. In this Transylvanian recipe, the eggs, white gold, reveal themselves as treasure within the deeply fragrant, dense meat.

1 tbsp sunflower oil

5 eggs

100g/3½oz/scant ½ cup long-grain white rice, rinsed and drained

60g/2¼oz smoked bacon, diced

2 onions, chopped

1 tbsp chopped parsley leaves

450g/1lb finely minced/ ground beef

450g/1lb finely minced/ ground pork

1½ tsp salt

¼ tsp freshly ground black pepper

½ tsp dried majoram

180ml/6fl oz/¾ cup passata/ sieved tomatoes or tomato juice

Preheat the oven to 180°C/350°F/Gas 5. Brush the inside of a 900g/2lb loaf pan with the oil.

Put 3 of the eggs in a saucepan, cover with cold water and bring to the boil. Cook for 6–8 minutes, then transfer to a colander and cool quickly under cold running water. Shell and leave to one side.

Put the rice and 240ml/8fl oz/1 cup water in a small saucepan, and bring to the boil over a medium-high heat. Turn the heat down to medium-low and simmer for 5 minutes. Drain in a colander and rinse with cold water to stop the cooking process. Leave to one side.

Fry the bacon in a frying pan until it has rendered the fat. Then stir in the onions and parsley and cook until the onions wilt and the bacon turns golden.

Combine the minced/ground beef and pork in a separate bowl. Add the bacon, onions and all the fat and scrapings from the pan and mix well. Add the rice, salt, pepper, marjoram, passata/sieved tomatoes to this meat and bacon mixture, then work in the remaining 2 eggs. Use your hands to knead it all thoroughly.

Pack one-third of the meat mixture into the prepared loaf pan. Now lay the shelled hard-boiled eggs lengthways down the middle and cover with the rest of the meat. Score the top of the loaf in a diamond pattern and put in the oven.

Bake for 1 hour, or until the meat has shrunk away from the sides of the tin. Remove from the oven and pour off any excess fat from the sides of the loaf. Allow the loaf to rest for 30 minutes.

Turn out the loaf, carve into thick slices and serve hot or cold.

Beefed-up bibimbap

Serves: 4
Prep: 20 minutes
Cook: 35 minutes

Traditionally served in hot stone bowls, this Korean speciality is positively encouraged towards a burnt rice bottom. I usually dive spoon-first, deep down to the stone-brown scrapings and count each topping I pick up, as I resurface, a blessing. To *bibimbap* properly you must *gochujang* – a thick, sweet Korean sauce, which brightens rice with its sweet, oriental tang. It is usually served with a fried egg on top, which is mashed ignominiously into the dish before serving.

225g/8oz/1¼ cups Thai fragrant rice, rinsed and drained

3 tbsp soy sauce

1½ tbsp rice vinegar

1½ tbsp caster/granulated sugar

3 garlic cloves, crushed

1½ tbsp toasted sesame oil

300g/10½oz rib-eye steak, thinly sliced

sunflower oil, for frying

115g/4oz/2 cups shiitake mushrooms, stems removed and finely sliced

2 small carrots, peeled and cut into fine matchsticks

150g/5½oz/1½ cups bean sprouts

300g/10½oz pak choi/bok choy, roughly chopped

4 tbsp gochujang (Korean chilli paste)

2 tsp sesame seeds

3 spring onions/scallions, finely sliced

salt and freshly ground black pepper

Put the rice in a saucepan with 455ml/16fl oz/2 cups water and a pinch of salt. Bring to the boil over a medium-high heat, then turn the heat down to medium and simmer for around 20 minutes. Once all the rice looks as though it has been absorbed, clamp on a tight lid and remove the pan from the heat.

Combine the soy sauce, rice vinegar, sugar, garlic and half the sesame oil in a mixing bowl and mix thoroughly until all the sugar dissolves. Add the sliced steak to this mixture and coat in the marinade. Leave to one side.

Heat a little sunflower oil in a wok over a medium-high heat. Toss in the shiitake mushrooms, drizzle with a little sesame oil and season with salt and pepper. Cook for 2 minutes, then remove them from the pan and leave to one side.

Now repeat this process with the carrots and the bean sprouts, adding each ingredient separately to the heated pan with a little sunflower oil and removing and setting each one aside to be combined later.

Finally, cook the pak choi/bok choy in the same way, adding half the gochujang sauce. Add half of the sesame seeds and the remaining sesame oil. Toss for 2 minutes until the pak choi/bok choy is wilted.

Heat a little oil in a wok over a medium-high heat until hot. Add the marinated steak and cook for 2–4 minutes, or until the liquid has evaporated and the steak is cooked through.

Divide the rice among serving bowls. Top each bowl of rice with a quarter of the steak and a quarter of each of the vegetables. They should be arranged over the top of the rice in a pie-chart formation, each colour segment butted up to the next. Sprinkle with the sliced spring onions/scallions and sprinkle with the remaining sesame seeds. Serve hot with the remaining gochujang sauce on the side.

Lamb coriander koftas

Serves: 4
Prep: 20 minutes
Cook: 25 minutes

When Asians have minced/ground lamb in their refrigerator, they often default to these spiced meatballs. They are wonderfully simple in that they are basically a construction job. They go with flatbreads conventionally, yes, but add them to a sauce of your concoction and make yourself a meatball curry with the excess. These koftas just keep on giving.

125g/4½oz/⅔ cup white basmati rice, rinsed and drained
1 white onion, diced
2.5cm/1in piece of fresh root ginger, peeled and finely grated
1–2 green chillies, deseeded and finely chopped
50g/1¾oz/heaped ⅓ cup pitted dried dates
2 garlic cloves, crushed
2 tbsp olive oil
30g/1oz/1 cup very finely chopped mint leaves
30g/1oz/1 cup very finely chopped coriander/cilantro leaves
500g/1lb 2oz minced/ground lamb
1 tsp garam masala
1½ tsp ground cumin
2 tbsp tomato purée/paste
juice of ¼ lemon
salt and freshly ground black pepper
flatbreads and yogurt dip

In a heavy-based saucepan, bring 480ml/16fl oz/2 cups water to the boil over a medium-high heat. Add the rice and cook for 6–8 minutes, then drain it and set it aside.

Blitz the onion, ginger, chillies, dates and garlic in a food processor until roughly chopped.

Heat 1 tablespoon of the olive oil in a frying pan, add the onion and ginger mixture and fry for 5 minutes over a medium-low heat, or until translucent and fragrant.

Transfer the fried onion mixture to a large mixing bowl and add the chopped herbs, the meat, spices, tomato purée/paste, lemon juice and rice. Season with salt and pepper. Spend 5 minutes kneading and combining the mixture well, making sure the spices and ingredients are evenly distributed. With your hands, shape twelve 7cm/2¾in long oval koftas. Brush well with oil.

Heat a little oil in a frying pan over a medium heat. Add the koftas and cook, turning frequently, for 8 minutes, or until cooked through.

Serve with a cooling yogurt dip and flatbreads.

Rubble & squeak

Serves: 4
Prep: 20 minutes
Cook: 45 minutes

A control-freaky Italian student housemate of mine put much effort into his rarely successful evenings of wooing. Clothed in Armani lounge gear, in a fog of Old Spice, he would create his glory dishes of smooth-as-Barry-White risotto served with a crisp green salad. It was the morning after that excited me most. Usually in a haze of thwarted *amour*, he would transform his misfired risottos into the most stunning rubble and squeak cakes. 'It's what my mamma taught me,' he flounced – in lieu of social skills, it seemed.

THE SALMON AND SAFFRON RISOTTO

8 saffron strands
75g/2½oz/5 tbsp butter
1 onion, finely chopped
280g/10oz/1½ cups risotto rice, rinsed and drained
1.2 litres/40fl oz/5 cups hot chicken stock
80g/2¾oz/heaped 1 cup freshly grated Parmesan cheese
350g/12oz salmon fillet, finely sliced
salt and freshly ground black pepper

THE RICE CAKES

1 tbsp chopped parsley leaves
1 tbsp snipped chives
1 tsp chopped dill, plus extra to serve
1 egg, lightly beaten
4 tbsp ground rice, plus extra for dusting
olive oil, for frying

Put the saffron strands in a small bowl, just cover with hot water and leave to steep for 10 minutes.

Heat half the butter in a saucepan and fry the onion until softened. Add the rice and stir for about 4 minutes.

Now begin to add the stock, a ladleful at a time, stirring over a low heat until all the liquid is absorbed before adding any more. Add the saffron and its soaking water. The risotto should be creamy and moist and have absorbed all the stock within about 20 minutes.

Stir in the remaining butter and the Parmesan. As soon as this has melted into the risotto, add the salmon slices. Stir very gently and cook for 2 more minutes until the fish is just cooked through. Remove from the heat immediately. Season with salt and pepper to taste, then – if you are just serving the risotto – serve hot with a twist of sharpening black pepper on top.

Make the rubble and squeak from the cooled risotto or any leftovers. To the cooled risotto mix, add the chopped herbs and the beaten egg. Now stir in enough rice flour to bind the mixture. It should remain soft but malleable. Dust your hands with extra ground rice and shape the mixture into patties about 13cm/5in in diameter and 2cm/¾in thick.

Heat the oil in a shallow pan and fry the rice cakes in batches for 4–5 minutes over a medium-low heat. Each side needs to be evenly browned. Remove and drain on paper towels, then allow to cool a little and serve sprinkled with chopped dill.

Serves: 4
Prep: 20 minutes
Cook: 15 minutes

Zingy pineapple & anchovy arancini

Okay, so this recipe might see Italian mommas crying into their ragu in horror, but this zingy pineapple anchovy combination is a source of sweet-and-sour-dipping-sauce joy to millions of Vietnamese. I confess, I have tried and tried but I have struggled to make really good arancini. I expect so much ooze and umph from these crisp, unassuming little balls, I had to go this far off piste to get there. For both my tyrannical palate and my brazen adulteration of this Italian classic, I beg your forgiveness. Try them, though, to properly seal your smirking contempt.

30g/1oz pineapple

1 tsp butter

¼ small red chilli, deseeded and finely chopped

1 tsp soft brown sugar

a squeeze of lime juice

5 anchovy fillets in oil, drained

rapeseed/canola or sunflower oil, for deep-frying and oiling

½ recipe quantity cold leftover Parmesan, Sage & Riesling Risotto (see page 169)

60g/2¼oz good (but not buffalo) mozzarella cheese, cubed

55g/2oz/scant ½ cup plain/all-purpose flour

1 egg, beaten

100g/3½oz/1¼ cups dried breadcrumbs

Blitz the pineapple in a food processor.

Heat the butter in a small frying pan over a medium heat until just smoking. Add the chilli, sugar, lime juice and pineapple and cook for 1–2 minutes until the juices combine and begin to thicken a little. Remove the pan from the heat.

Roughly mash the anchovy fillets into the cooked pineapple purée with the back of a teaspoon and keep aside in a bowl.

Rub a little oil onto your hands. Take a tablespoon of risotto into your palm and flatten it into a disc. Put a cube of mozzarella and ¼ teaspoon of the anchovy pineapple mix in the middle of the disc and press the risotto gently around the mixture to form a firm ball. Repeat this process until all the risotto is used up. You should have 16 balls.

Now roll the balls in the flour. Transfer them to the beaten egg, covering them quickly. Then roll them in the breadcrumbs and set on a plate.

Heat the deep-frying oil in a large wok over a medium-high heat. Test the heat by dropping in a few breadcrumbs. When they fizz quickly up to the top, the oil is at the right temperature. Now gently lower the arancini into the oil in small batches and fry for about 5 minutes until golden brown. Remove with a slotted spoon and drain on paper towels.

Serve hot – but not to your Italian mother-in-law.

Sushi rice

It was only when I watched Nigella Lawson prodding away at hallowed sushi rice smothered in Korean jarred paste, probably in a dressing gown with her feet up, that I considered myself worthy of this grain. It's a short-grained, white Japanese rice and is dressed with rice vinegar, sugar and salt for sushi. This is what gives it that sweet, zingy, gentle hum that seems almost intrinsic to the rice grain. This combination of unlikely companions is a stroke of Japanese rice-cooking genius.

It is stickier than other rices, but apart from that there is no need to fear it. To me it's a good half-way house between nutty long-grain and all-out sticky rice. It's just adhesive enough to act as a sort of rice trencher, a sweet, sturdy bed to hold a full-bodied sauce. Chopstick-based culinary cultures like the good and sticky grain.

Sushi rice bought in Japan has already been treated with sugar, salt and vinegar. In the West, popular types of sushi rice are Kokuho Rose, Calrose, and Japanese Rose. An economical alternative is the round, pearl-like dongbei rice. It is good and sticky, with a little of the required sweetness.

How to cook sushi rice

* Use 1 cup of rice to 1¼ cups of water (190g/6¾oz rice to 300ml/10½fl oz water).

* Put the rice in a colander and rinse under cold running water until the water runs clear. Leave to drain.

* Put the rice and water in a saucepan and bring to the boil, then simmer for about 15 minutes, uncovered, until almost dry with a dimpled surface.

* Cover tightly, remove from the heat and leave to stand for 15 minutes.

To use the rice for sushi

* Cook 3 cups of rice in 3¾ cups of water, as above.

* In a separate pan, heat 80ml/2½fl oz/⅓ cup rice vinegar, 3 tablespoons sugar and 1 teaspoon salt.

* Turn the cooked rice onto a wide, non-metallic dish and sprinkle over the sweet vinegar mix. Use a rice spatula to gently fold the flavour into the rice. The quicker you cool and dry this dish, the glossier the rice grains will be. The use of a fan is not going too far, believe it or not.

Sweet squid sushi fix

For me, sushi rice does this rather remarkable sweet, tangy, body temperature thing like nothing else. Against the luxurious comfort of the rice, I love the fight and fragrance of the sweet aromatic squid. Chop a few bird's eye chillies in if you want to go hotter, as heaven forbid any corner of your mouth go unstimulated while chasing the sushi squid dragon.

280g/10oz/scant 2 cups sushi rice

5 tbsp rice vinegar

1 tbsp sugar

½ tsp fine sea salt

THE SQUID

2 tbsp tamarind paste

2 tbsp lime juice

1½ tbsp Asian fish sauce

2 garlic cloves, crushed

1 tbsp caster/granulated sugar

1 tbsp sweet chilli sauce

1 small red onion, finely sliced

1 handful of coriander/cilantro leaves, chopped, plus extra leaves to serve

1 handful of mint leaves, chopped

500g/1lb 2oz large squid, cleaned

1 tsp salt

Put the rice in a large colander and rinse with cold water until the water runs clear. Leave the rice to drain for 15 minutes.

Put the rice in a saucepan and cover with 570ml/20fl oz/2½ cups cold water and bring to the boil over a medium-high heat. Reduce the heat to low, cover and simmer for 15 minutes. Remove from the heat and leave to stand, covered, for 15 minutes.

Meanwhile, bring the vinegar to a simmer in a small saucepan. Remove from the heat and whisk in the sugar and salt until dissolved. Put the vinegar mixture and the rice in a large bowl and toss to combine. Leave to cool completely.

Stir the tamarind paste into 60ml/2fl oz/¼ cup warm water. Add the lime juice, fish sauce, garlic, sugar, chilli sauce, onion, coriander/cilantro and mint leaves. Stir well until the sugar has dissolved.

Cut the squid into strips and lightly score the non-membraneous side of the strips in a criss-cross. Halve the tentacles.

Bring a large saucepan of water to the boil with the salt. Drop the squid into the water and cook for 45 seconds or just until it turns white. Drain in a colander, then rinse under cold water to stop the cooking process. Add the squid to the sauce and toss well.

Spoon the squid over the sushi rice and drizzle with the sauce. Sprinkle with coriander/cilantro leaves and serve immediately.

Funky fish fingers

Well, they are croquettes really but I cannot resist the alliteration. These have a real Japanese twist. You don't need to use sushi rice but feel free. You're aiming for all the internal sweet tang and flesh of sushi with a satisfying crunching heft in the crisp panko coating.

Serves: 4
Prep: 30 minutes, plus standing and chilling
Cook: 130 minutes

350g/12oz cod fillet, thinly
sliced
1 tbsp salt
115g/4oz/scant ⅔ cup
short-grain white rice,
rinsed and drained

THE FISH DRESSING
5 tbsp rice vinegar
2 tsp caster/granulated sugar
1 tsp salt
3 eggs
2 tbsp finely chopped spring
onions/scallions or chives
rapeseed/canola or
sunflower oil, for deep-
frying and oiling
115g/4oz/2½ cups panko
breadcrumbs
tartare sauce and lemon
wedges

Sprinkle the fish with the salt in a bowl, toss lightly and leave to stand for 30 minutes. Rinse well with cold water.

Put the rice and 350ml/12fl oz/1½ cups water in a saucepan, bring to the boil, then turn the heat down and cook over a medium heat until all the water has been absorbed. Now switch off the heat, cover the pan and leave for 15 minutes.

Mix the rice vinegar, sugar and salt in a small saucepan. Bring to the boil and boil for 2 minutes, making sure the sugar and salt have dissolved. Leave to cool slightly.

Transfer the rice to a large mixing bowl. Add the cooled vinegar to the warm rice, then leave to cool completely.

Add the slices of fish to the cold rice with one whole egg and the spring onions/scallions and mix well, using your hand to ensure you get an even mix of ingredients.

Wash your hands, then rub them with a little oil. Using your hands, shape the mixture into croquette shapes 4–5cm/1½–2in long. You should get about 16. Put on a tray and refrigerate for at least 30 minutes.

Lightly beat the remaining eggs in a shallow dish. Spread the panko breadcrumbs on a separate tray. Remove the fish fingers from the refrigerator.

Heat the oil in a wok to a medium-high heat. Test the temperature by dropping in a few breadcrumbs. If they fizz and cook quickly, the oil is ready. Dip each fish finger into the egg, then roll it in the breadcrumbs.

Fry the fish fingers in small batches for about 5 minutes until golden brown. Drain on paper towels before serving with lemon wedges and tartare sauce.

Tea-steeped chickpea pot

Serves: 4
Prep: 10 minutes,
plus steeping
Cook: 40 minutes

This is one of India's favourite go-to comfort dishes. It is traditionally served with bhatura or puri – classic Indian deep-fried breads. 'You should open a restaurant and serve just this and puri,' barked my ma, 'and you will do very well, mark my words.' So I did, and tea-steeped chickpeas are one of our biggest sellers.

1 tbsp strong tea leaves

1½ tbsp sunflower oil

2 onions, finely diced

2.5cm/1in piece of fresh root ginger, peeled and grated

1 garlic clove, crushed

1–2 green finger chillies, deseeded and finely chopped

1 tsp soft brown sugar

1 tsp turmeric

½ tsp ground cumin

1½ tsp garam masala

¼ tsp chilli powder

100g/3½oz/scant ½ cup white basmati rice, rinsed and drained

400g/14oz can chopped tomatoes

400g/14oz can chickpeas, drained

25g/1oz baby leaf spinach

a handful of coriander/ cilantro leaves, roughly chopped

salt and freshly ground black pepper

thick plain yogurt

Boil 480ml/16fl oz/2 cups water and add it to the tea leaves. Leave to steep.

Heat the oil in a large heavy-based pan. Add the onions, ginger and garlic and cook over a medium-high heat until the onions are browned and sweet. Add the green chillies, brown sugar, turmeric, cumin, garam masala and chilli powder. Cook over a medium heat for 1 minute.

Now add the rice and stir over a medium heat for 2 minutes until all the grains are covered with the spice mix. Add the tomatoes and simmer over a medium-low heat for 5 minutes.

Add the chickpeas. Strain the steeped tea and add the liquor to the pan. Season with salt and pepper. Simmer, uncovered, over a low heat for 15–20 minutes until the rice is fully tender.

Stir in the whole baby spinach leaves until they turn into soft green ribbons through the dish.

Sprinkle with the chopped coriander/cilantro leaves, season with salt and pepper and serve hot with a dollop of thick plain yogurt.

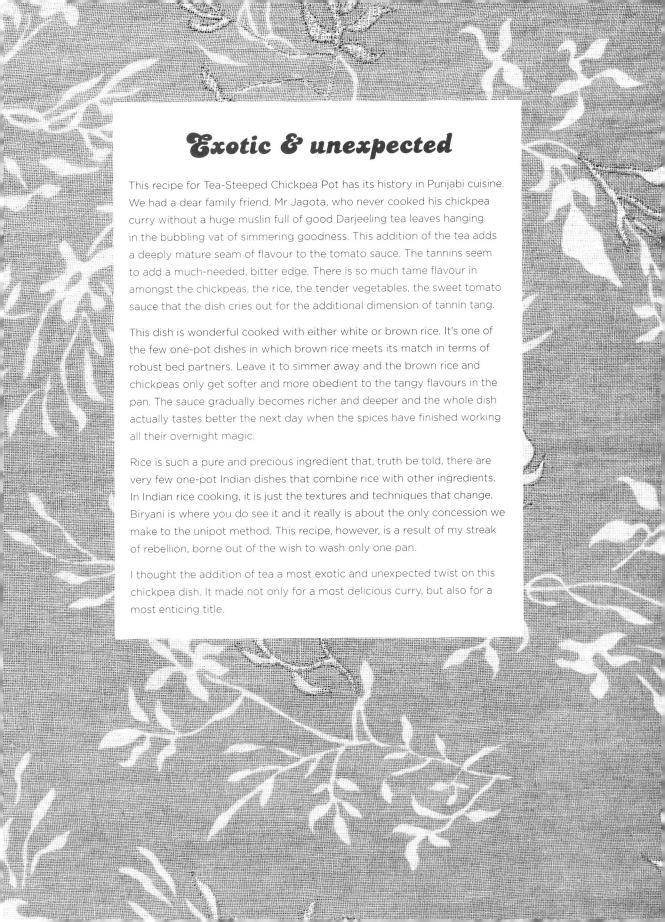

Exotic & unexpected

This recipe for Tea-Steeped Chickpea Pot has its history in Punjabi cuisine. We had a dear family friend, Mr Jagota, who never cooked his chickpea curry without a huge muslin full of good Darjeeling tea leaves hanging in the bubbling vat of simmering goodness. This addition of the tea adds a deeply mature seam of flavour to the tomato sauce. The tannins seem to add a much-needed, bitter edge. There is so much tame flavour in amongst the chickpeas, the rice, the tender vegetables, the sweet tomato sauce that the dish cries out for the additional dimension of tannin tang.

This dish is wonderful cooked with either white or brown rice. It's one of the few one-pot dishes in which brown rice meets its match in terms of robust bed partners. Leave it to simmer away and the brown rice and chickpeas only get softer and more obedient to the tangy flavours in the pan. The sauce gradually becomes richer and deeper and the whole dish actually tastes better the next day when the spices have finished working all their overnight magic.

Rice is such a pure and precious ingredient that, truth be told, there are very few one-pot Indian dishes that combine rice with other ingredients. In Indian rice cooking, it is just the textures and techniques that change. Biryani is where you do see it and it really is about the only concession we make to the unipot method. This recipe, however, is a result of my streak of rebellion, borne out of the wish to wash only one pan.

I thought the addition of tea a most exotic and unexpected twist on this chickpea dish. It made not only for a most delicious curry, but also for a most enticing title.

Red rice gado gado

Okay, I know the sauce looks complicated but this dish is so utterly tantalizing it is worth cracking it at least once in your life. After all, everyone should have a killer peanut sauce in their armoury. It is an Eastern gift of excess, to be able to create such virtuosity and relegate it to a sauce. The resoundingly dull salad ingredients form a critically bland foil for the bite of the rice and the song of the sauce.

THE PEANUT SAUCE

4 garlic cloves

1 lemongrass stalk, chopped

2cm/¾in piece of galangal

2 shallots, chopped

2 tbsp sunflower oil

3 tsp toasted shrimp paste

200g/7oz/1½ cups roasted
   peanuts, finely chopped

1 tbsp salt

55g/2oz/¼ cup palm sugar

1 tbsp sweet soy sauce

2 tsp paprika

1 tbsp tamarind paste

200ml/7fl oz/scant 1 cup
   coconut milk

juice of 1 lime

½ red Thai chilli (optional)

THE RED RICE

100g/3½oz/heaped ½ cup
   red rice, preferably Thai,
   rinsed and drained

a pinch of salt

2 garlic cloves, crushed

THE POTATO & BEAN SALAD

2 potatoes, peeled

55g/2oz/1 cup bean sprouts

100g/3½oz French beans,
   trimmed and halved

½ cucumber, thickly sliced

4 hard-boiled eggs

100g/3½oz tofu, sliced

2 tbsp coriander/cilantro leaves

Put the rice in a large bowl and pour in enough water to cover it by 2.5cm/1in. Leave to soak for 30 minutes.

To make the sauce, grind the garlic, lemongrass, galangal and shallots to a paste in a food processor.

Heat the oil in a saucepan, add the shrimp paste and cook over a low heat for around 5 minutes. You are waiting for the oil to rise to the top.

Reserve 1 teaspoon of the peanuts and add the remainder to the pan with the spice paste, the shrimp paste, salt, sugar, soy sauce and paprika. Dissolve the tamarind in a little water, then add it to the pan and simmer for 10 minutes over a medium-low heat. Finally stir in the coconut milk and leave to one side.

Drain the rice, then tip it into a saucepan with the salt, garlic and 240ml/8fl oz/1 cup water. Bring to the boil over a medium-high heat, then turn the heat down to low, cover and simmer for about 15 minutes until the rice is soft and cooked through.

Meanwhile, to make the salad, cut the potatoes into wedges, put in a large heavy-based pan and cover with water. Bring to the boil over a medium-high heat, boil for 10 minutes until just soft, then drain and put aside.

Add 1 litre/35fl oz/4⅓ cups water to the pan, keep the heat medium-high and return the water to the boil. Drop in the bean sprouts and cook for about 30 seconds, then remove with a slotted spoon. Add the beans into the same boiling water and remove after about 5 minutes, when tender.

To serve the dish, put the rice in the form of a bed on a large serving plate. Add the cooked vegetables, the cucumber and tofu slices. Quarter the eggs and lay them on the top, then sit a small bowl of peanut sauce in the dish, or pour it over the top if you prefer. Drizzle the lime juice over the top and sprinkle with the chilli, if you like, then finish with the coriander/cilantro leaves and the reserved peanuts.

Ricotta rammed 'rooms

In some pastoral communities across the globe, these are known as shepherd's mushrooms because of the ricotta salute to sheep. Lemon and garlic coax zing and flavour into the thudding ricotta and earthy mushrooms, which, let's face it, are some of the more lacklustre ingredients to be found in a far-flung goatskin kitchen tent.

55g/2oz/scant ⅓ cup long-grain brown rice, preferably basmati, soaked for 2 hours, rinsed and drained
180ml/6fl oz/¾ cup vegetable stock
1 garlic clove, very finely chopped
300g/10½oz medium-size mushrooms
185g/6½oz smoked bacon cut into small cubes
1 tbsp oil
250g/9oz/generous 1 cup ricotta cheese
2 tsp lemon juice
zest of ½ lemon
4 tbsp thyme leaves
salt and freshly ground black pepper
green salad and crostini

Put the rice, stock and garlic in a saucepan and bring slowly to the boil, then cover and cook very gently for 20–25 minutes until the rice is tender. Remove the pan from the heat, cover and leave for 15 minutes.

Preheat the oven to 180°C/350°F/Gas 4 and grease a baking sheet.

Remove the stalks from the mushrooms. Arrange the mushrooms on the prepared baking sheet, gill-side up.

Fry the bacon in the oil in a non-stick pan over a medium-high heat until golden brown. Remove the bacon and put in a bowl to cool.

Stir the bacon into the rice, then add the ricotta cheese, lemon juice, lemon zest and thyme and season with salt and pepper. Mix well to combine. Spoon generously into the prepared mushroom caps.

Bake the stuffed mushrooms for 10–12 minutes or until the cheese mixture is golden. Remove and serve with a green salad and crostini.

Belting bhajis

Serves: 4
Prep: 10 minutes
Cook: 15 minutes

Forgive the obtuse link to rice, but the rice flour does have such a transformative effect on the levity and crispness of the bhajis that it is far from a contrived inclusion.

2 tbsp rice flour

200g/7oz/1⅔ cups gram flour

½ tsp ground coriander

½ tsp ground cumin

2 tbsp finely chopped coriander/cilantro

2 garlic cloves, crushed

2 mild green chillies, deseeded and finely chopped

1 tsp ajwain seeds (optional)

1 tsp salt

1 tsp freshly ground black pepper

¼ tsp bicarbonate of soda/ baking soda

sunflower oil, for deep-frying

3 medium or small onions, sliced into 1cm/½in rings

chutney or yogurt dip

Combine the flours, spices, coriander/cilantro, garlic, chillies and ajwain seeds, if using, salt, pepper and bicarbonate of soda in a large mixing bowl and mix thoroughly. Add 300ml/10½fl oz/1¼ cups warm water and mix together to form a smooth, loose batter.

Heat the frying oil in a large wok over a high heat. Check the temperature has reached frying heat by dropping a touch of batter into the hot oil. It should bubble and float to the surface in a few seconds, golden brown, if the oil is at the right temperature.

Toss a small batch of the onion rings into the batter, making sure they are fully coated.

Transfer the battered rings to the hot oil and cook for 2 minutes. Turn and fry for a further 3 minutes until they are evenly golden brown. Remove from the oil and drain on paper towels. Repeat in small batches, then serve hot with a good chutney or yogurt dip.

Peanut ping pongs

These nutty little dipping balls rely quite heavily on the dipping sauce partners to bring them to full life. Not many recipes involve the blitzing of cooked rice to a paste. It can cause a little panic but go with it. Usually when I scan a recipe, I can see the area of the world it came from by certain iconic ingredients. The soy and ginger would have made you think China, but the ground coriander is a confusion. Sichuan province is where they bowl such googlies.

115g/4oz/⅔ cup basmati or other long-grain white rice, rinsed and drained (or use 225g/8oz/1⅔ cups cooked rice)

1 garlic clove, crushed

1cm/½in piece of fresh root ginger, peeled and grated

1 tsp caster/granulated sugar

1½ tsp salt

1 small green chilli, deseeded and chopped

2 tsp light soy sauce

2 tbsp chopped coriander/cilantro leaves

½ tsp ground coriander

juice of ½ lime

115g/4oz/heaped ¾ cup skinless peanuts, chopped

rapeseed/canola or sunflower oil, for deep-frying

1 lime, cut into 4 wedges, and chilli dipping sauce

Put the rice in a saucepan and pour in 320ml/11fl oz/1⅓ cups water. Bring slowly to the boil, then cover and cook very gently for 20–25 minutes until the rice is tender. Remove the pan from the heat and leave, covered, until cool. Alternatively, you can use cooked leftover rice.

Blitz the garlic, ginger, sugar, salt, chilli, soy sauce, coriander/cilantro, ground coriander and lime juice in a food processor until the mixture becomes a thick paste. Add three-quarters of the cooked rice and process again until you have a smooth, sticky paste. Transfer this mixture to a large mixing bowl and stir in the rest of the rice.

Put the chopped peanuts on a plate.

Wet your hands and roll small balls of the rice mix in your palms. They should be around 2–3cm/¾–1¼in in diameter and you should get about 16 balls out of the mixture. Roll the balls in the chopped peanuts, making sure they are evenly coated.

Heat the oil in a deep pan or wok and test the oil by dropping in a piece of peanut. If it sizzles, the oil is at the right temperature. Now drop in the peanut balls, in batches if necessary, and fry for a few minutes until they become brown and crisp. Remove and drain on paper towels.

Serve hot as finger food with the lime wedges and chilli dipping sauce.

Feta nut fritters

Serves: 4
Prep: 20 minutes
Cook: 35 minutes

These are great little snacks, quick to make and super for using up leftover rice. The cheese can be too strong, I feel, so make sure you have no more than two-thirds cheese to one-third rice proportion. That should make sure they are quite intense in flavour with the tang of the feta peeking resiliently above the taming starch of the rice and dark toasting of the nuts. Try them with a crisp green salad.

65g/2¼oz/⅓ cup risotto or
  other short-grain white rice,
  rinsed and drained
3 egg whites
350g/12oz feta cheese, finely
  crumbled
4 tsp thyme leaves
4 tbsp fresh breadcrumbs
1 tbsp hazelnuts
3 tbsp olive oil
½ tbsp butter
salt and freshly ground black
  pepper

Put the rice in a saucepan and pour in 175ml/6fl oz/¾ cup water. Bring slowly to the boil, then cover and cook very gently for 20–25 minutes until the rice is tender. Remove the pan from the heat and leave to the side, covered, until cool.

Whisk the egg whites in a clean grease-free bowl until they form stiff peaks. Carefully fold in the crumbled cheese and rice. Season to taste with salt and pepper, and gently mix in the thyme. Shape the mixture into about 16 small balls.

Toss the hazelnuts in a hot pan until lightly toasted, then chop finely and tip into a bowl. Add the breadcrumbs and mix well. Roll each of the cheese balls in the mixture and put on a baking sheet.

Heat the oil and butter in a large non-stick pan and, when hot, add the cheese balls and sauté for 2–3 minutes, turning them frequently, until golden brown all over. Remove from the heat, drain on paper towels and serve hot.

Serves: 4
Prep: 40 minutes,
plus chilling
Cook: 30 minutes

Spiced spinach spheres

These are fragrant, crisp little rice fritters. The spinach and bacon add depth of flavour. The garlic and thyme give high notes of herbal zing. These are a kind of pintxo snack, Northern Spanish in structure but swinging East in flavour. I love ground coriander, herbal and citrus. Those flavours, along with the fresh thyme, make these fried spheres feel light and fresh.

300g/10½oz/heaped 1½ cups Thai fragrant rice or other short-grain rice, rinsed and drained

900g/2lb baby leaf spinach, stalks removed

2 tbsp olive oil

3 onions, finely sliced

6 garlic cloves, 2 crushed and 4 finely chopped

150g/5½oz lean bacon, finely diced

3 tbsp rice flour

2 tsp ground coriander

1 tbsp thyme leaves

juice of ½ lemon

¼ tsp cayenne pepper

2 eggs, separated

oil, for deep-frying and oiling

100g/3½oz/1⅓ cups fresh breadcrumbs

¼ tsp freshly grated nutmeg

salt and freshly ground black pepper

chutneys or yogurt dip

Bring the rice to the boil with 700ml/24fl oz/3 cups water. Turn the heat down to medium-low and simmer for 15 minutes, or until all the water has been absorbed. Clamp on a tight lid and remove from the heat. Leave the pan to cool thoroughly.

Cover the spinach with lightly salted boiling water in a large pan and boil for 2 minutes. Drain and rinse with cold water. Squeeze out the excess water, chop roughly and leave to one side.

Heat the olive oil in a heavy-based frying pan and fry the onions, crushed and chopped garlic and the bacon for 4 minutes. Remove from the pan and drain on paper towels. Leave to cool.

Mix the onion mixture with the cooked rice and rice flour, then add the spinach, ground coriander, thyme leaves, lemon juice, cayenne, egg yolks and salt and pepper and mix thoroughly. Use your hands and knead until you feel the rice and spinach mixture become sticky.

Rub your hands with a little cooking oil and begin to form about 20 small balls with the rice mixture, each about 4cm/1½in in diameter. Put them on a tray lined with cling film/plastic wrap. Refrigerate for at least 30 minutes.

Beat the egg whites lightly in a large bowl. Pour the breadcrumbs onto a large plate and season with salt, pepper and nutmeg.

Remove the spinach balls from the refrigerator and roll each one first in the egg white, then onto the plate of breadcrumbs.

Bring the oil to a high heat in a large wok. Test the oil by dropping in a small amount of mixture. If it sizzles, the oil is ready. Deep-fry the balls in batches for 5 minutes until browned and crisp.

Serve hot or warm with your favourite chutneys or a yogurt dip.

Spinach sweetcorn soufflé-ish

This sweet-textured, stand-alone soufflé-style dish makes a great accompaniment to a host of mains, but when served with a salad and crusty bread, frankly, it can steal centre stage.

Serves: 4
Prep: 20 minutes, plus standing
Cook: 1 hour 10 minutes

95g/3¼oz/ ½ cup white long-grain rice, rinsed and drained (or use 170g/6oz/1¼ cups cooked rice)
450g/1lb/4 cups baby spinach leaves, washed thoroughly
1 tbsp sunflower oil, plus extra for greasing
2 onions, chopped
2 garlic cloves, finely chopped
1 tsp ground coriander
½ tsp ground cumin
225g/8oz/2¼ cups sweetcorn, blended to a purée
75g/2½oz mature/sharp Cheddar cheese
4 eggs, beaten
salt and freshly ground black pepper

Put the rice in a saucepan with 240ml/8fl oz/1 cup water, bring to the boil and simmer gently for 15 minutes until most of the water has been absorbed. Remove from the heat, cover tightly and leave for 15 minutes. Alternatively, you can use cooked, leftover rice.

Blanch the spinach leaves in boiling water for 1 minute, drain, squeeze out the excess water and chop. Leave to one side.

Pour the oil into a heavy-based frying pan and fry the onions and garlic over a medium heat until soft. Add the ground coriander and cumin and cook for 1 minute.

Add the sweetcorn purée, cheese and eggs and stir in the cooked rice. Combine well and season with salt and pepper. Stir in the chopped spinach and ensure it is evenly mixed in.

Generously oil the inside of a 1 litre/35fl oz/4⅓ cup pudding basin or similar mould. Transfer the rice and spinach mixture and press it down into the basin. Cover with foil and put the basin in a saucepan. Pour hot water into the saucepan so that it comes halfway up the outside of the basin. Cover the pan and bring the water to the boil. Once boiled, lower the heat to medium-low and simmer, still covered, for 40–50 minutes until the mixture is risen and just set. It should have a slight wobble but, if in doubt, a skewer or knife inserted in the middle should come out clean.

Preheat the oven to 200°C/400°F/Gas 6.

Remove the basin from the hot water and leave the pudding to stand for 10 minutes, then run a palette knife around the inside of the basin. Put a plate over the basin and turn it over and out on to an ovenproof serving dish. Put in the oven for 10 minutes just until the top becomes golden, then serve warm.

3

Main grains

Fantastic feasts from around the world

Boozy Japanese claypot chicken

Serves: 4
Prep: 30 minutes, plus marinating
Cook: 45 minutes

The anticipation on lifting the lid on a clay pot dish is fever pitch. So much is demanded from so little by so many – we want earthy, we want filling and we want a thing of rustic beauty. They might be a pain to get hold of, but the funkier the mushrooms, the more the earthy and beauty boxes are ticked.

450g/1lb skinless, boneless chicken thighs, cut into cubes

2 tsp dark soy sauce

2 tbsp oyster sauce

6 dried porcini mushrooms

4 tbsp sunflower oil

4 anchovies

4 garlic cloves, finely chopped

2 tbsp finely chopped fresh root ginger

200g/7oz/1¼ cups long-grain white rice, rinsed and drained

200g/7oz butternut squash, peeled, deseeded and cut into cubes

6 chestnut/cremini mushrooms, sliced

250ml/9fl oz/generous 1 cup any Japanese-style beer

4 baby pak choi/bok choy, ends trimmed

2 red chillies, deseeded and sliced

2 tbsp chopped coriander/cilantro leaves (optional)

Marinate the chicken in the soy sauce and oyster sauce for 30 minutes.

Soak the porcini mushrooms in warm water for about 15 minutes until soft. Drain, reserving the soaking liquid. Discard any hard or gritty bits and chop the mushrooms roughly.

Heat 1 tablespoon of the oil in a clay pot or a large flameproof casserole and add the anchovies. Fry them on a brisk heat until they melt.

Add the garlic and ginger and as they begin to soften, turn the heat down to medium. Add the rice, butternut squash and chestnut/cremini mushrooms and toss into this fragrant oil.

Pour in the Japanese beer, then top up with 4 tablespoons of the water used to soak the porcini mushrooms and about 200ml/7fl oz/scant 1 cup water so the liquid is 2.5cm/1in above the surface of the rice. Toss in the porcini mushrooms, cover the clay pot and simmer for about 10 minutes until the rice and squash are nearly cooked through.

Now drain and add the marinated chicken, arranging it on top of the rice. Carefully trickle the remaining oil around the inside surface of the pan to encourage a brown, crisp edge to the rice. Cover the pan and simmer gently for a further 15 minutes, then turn off the heat.

Add the pak choi/bok choy and re-cover the dish, leaving the clay pot to finish cooking with its own retained heat for a further 15 minutes.

Serve sprinkled with the sliced red chilli and the chopped coriander/cilantro leaves, if you like.

Serves: 4
Prep: 20 minutes
Cook: 1 hour
15 minutes

Pimped rice piri piri

This is a great way to send four chicken breasts a long way – all the way to the red pepper heat of Portugal.

280g/10oz/heaped 1½ cups
   long-grain white rice,
   rinsed and drained
4 skinless, boneless chicken
   breasts
3 tbsp olive oil
1 large onion, sliced
3 garlic cloves, chopped
2 red peppers, deseeded and
   sliced
2 yellow peppers, deseeded
   and sliced
4–8 red chillies, sliced (use
   less or more according to
   taste)
1 tsp dried thyme
½ tsp dried oregano
1 tbsp sweet smoked paprika
2 tomatoes, chopped
1 tbsp tomato purée/paste
1 litre/35fl oz/4⅓ cups
   chicken stock
3½ tbsp red wine vinegar
a few coriander/cilantro
   leaves
salt and freshly ground black
   pepper

Preheat the oven to 180°C/350°F/Gas 4.

Put the rice in an even layer in the bottom of a large ovenproof dish.

Season the chicken with salt and pepper. Heat 2 tbsp of the oil in a frying pan over a high heat and brown the chicken quickly on all sides, then put it on top of the rice in the ovenproof dish.

Add the remaining oil to the pan and fry the onions and garlic. Once softened, add the peppers and the as many of the chillies as you can bear. Fry for 5 minutes over a medium-low heat until the peppers are soft.

Add the thyme, oregano, smoked paprika, chopped tomatoes and tomato purée/paste. Stir briefly and season with salt and pepper to taste.

Now add the stock and red wine vinegar, bring to the boil, then simmer for 3 minutes. Pour this mixture over the chicken and rice. Cover tightly and transfer to the oven for 45 minutes until the rice and chicken are tender. Sprinkle with coriander/cilantro leaves and serve warm.

Serves: 4–6
Prep: 30 minutes
Cook: 1 hour 35 minutes

Pretty picnic pie

Leftover rice need not be forever relegated to the lacklustre cold salad. It wakes in Nirvana when teamed with luxurious freshly butter-poached chicken and creamy spiced baked yogurt.

280g/10oz/1½ cups white basmati rice, rinsed and drained

45g/1¾oz/3 tbsp salted butter, plus extra for finishing

1 large onion, diced

1.5kg/3lb 5oz skinless, boneless chicken breasts, cut into large chunks

1 tsp ground cumin

½ tsp ground cinnamon

240ml/8fl oz/1 cup chicken stock

480g/1lb 1oz/2 cups Greek yogurt

2 eggs, beaten

1½ tsp ground coriander

30g/1oz/¼ cup chopped pitted dates

55g/2oz/⅓ cup chopped apricots

50g/1¾oz/⅔ cup flaked/slivered almonds

salt and freshly ground black pepper

Add the rice to 700ml/24fl oz/3 cups boiling water, then simmer until the grains are soft, about 10 minutes. Leave to cool. Alternatively, use leftover cooked rice.

Add the butter to a frying pan over a medium-high heat, toss in the onion and the chicken pieces and fry until the pieces just begin to gain some colour. Add the cumin and cinnamon and cook for a further 2 minutes.

Add the stock, turn the heat down to medium-low and simmer until the stock has reduced by half. This usually takes about 30 minutes.

Combine the yogurt, eggs and coriander in a separate bowl and season with salt and pepper. Stir half of the rice into this yogurt mixture.

Preheat the oven to 160°C/315°F/Gas 2 and grease a 10cm/4in deep 20cm/8in baking dish.

Spoon the yogurt and rice mixture into the bottom of the baking dish. Remove the chicken pieces from the spiced stock reduction and arrange them on top of the rice and yogurt mix. Cover the chicken pieces with a thin layer of the remaining plain rice.

Sprinkle the chopped dates and apricots on top of this layer of rice. Then cover with the rest of the rice.

Pour the spiced chicken stock (from which you removed the chicken pieces) over the rice and sprinkle with the flaked/slivered almonds. Dot with a little butter, cover tightly with foil and bake for 35–45 minutes.

To help the pie to set, remove from the oven and stand the dish on a cold, damp dish towel to encourage the rice to lift from the bottom of the dish. Run a spatula or knife around the inside rim of the dish. Turn a large plate upside-down onto the top of the baking dish and turn the whole dish over, so turning out your rice cake.

Cut into wedges and serve hot or cold.

Jerked angry birds

A good jerk chicken is underpinned by the seasonings that come from the jerk trinity of allspice, Scotch bonnet and thyme. Think about where these flavours take you and up the amount as you wish. The masochist in me usually adds double the Scotch bonnet.

Serves: 4
Prep: 30 minutes,
plus marinating
Cook: 1 hour
plus marinating

4 boneless chicken breasts, skin on, flesh slashed

2 tbsp sunflower oil

2 small red onions, diced

2 garlic cloves, crushed

1 tsp soft brown sugar

1 celery stalk, finely chopped

1½ green or red peppers, deseeded and finely chopped

½ tsp dried thyme

2 spring onions/scallions, chopped

150g/5½oz/¾ cup long-grain white rice, rinsed and drained

400g/14oz can pinto beans, drained

2 tbsp tomato purée/paste

480ml/16fl oz/2 cups chicken stock

grated zest and juice of ½ lime

1 bunch of coriander/cilantro leaves, chopped

salt and freshly ground black pepper

1 lime, quartered

First, make the jerk sauce (see below). Add 2 tablespoons of the jerk sauce to the chicken breasts and rub it into the slashed flesh. Leave, covered, in the refrigerator for at least 2 hours and preferably overnight.

Heat the oil in a large heavy-based pan. Bring to a medium-high heat and add the chicken breasts, skin-side down. Turn after 2–3 minutes and cook the other side, ensuring both sides become brown and slightly crisp. Remove the chicken pieces from the pan and leave to one side.

Add the red onions and garlic to the oil in the pan and fry over a medium-high heat for 2–3 minutes. Add the brown sugar, celery, chopped green and red peppers, dried thyme and chopped spring onions/scallions. Cook over a medium heat for a further 5–7 minutes until the peppers soften. Now add the rice and toss it with the vegetable mix for 2–3 minutes. Add the beans, tomato purée/paste and stock and season with salt and pepper to taste. Cook over a medium-low heat for 5 minutes.

Return the chicken breasts to the pan, making sure they are tucked in amongst the swelling rice grains. Continue to cook over a medium-low heat for 15–20 minutes until the rice is completely cooked.

Add the lime zest and juice and stir carefully. Put a tightly fitting lid on the pan and cook for a further 5–10 minutes over a very low heat or until the chicken is cooked through. Leave the lid on and remove from the heat. Leave to rest for 10 minutes. Carefully transfer the chicken and rice mix to a serving plate, sprinkle with the chopped coriander/cilantro and top with lime wedges to serve.

THE JERK SAUCE

In a blender or food processor, blitz all these ingredients to a thick paste: ½ small red onion, 1 tsp salt, 1–2 orange Scotch bonnet chillies, deseeded, 1 tbsp thyme leaves, grated zest and juice of 1 lime, 2 tbsp light soy sauce, 2 tbsp olive oil, 3 tbsp muscovado/soft brown sugar, 1 tbsp ground allspice, 5 spring onions/scallions, roughly chopped, 2.5cm/1in fresh root ginger, peeled and chopped, 3 garlic cloves. Put in a screw-topped jar and keep in the refrigerator for up to 3 weeks.

Serves: 4-6
Prep: 20 minutes
Cook: 40 minutes

Dirty chicken rice

This Cajun favourite is the ultimate pimped-rice dish. The title alone makes it deliciously subversive. It is called 'dirty' because of the uncompromising offal colouring imparted by the liver. Here's funny; I'm allergic to chocolate and the closest I get to it in terms of texture and flavour is a good liver pâté: sweet, creamy, nutty depth. Go with it – the livers add a subtle, chocolate substratum to the rice.

2 tbsp sunflower oil

2 small onions, diced

3 garlic cloves, chopped

3 celery stalks, diced

1 red chilli, finely sliced
  (or half, depending on how
  hot you want it)

2 green peppers, deseeded
  and diced

100g/3½oz chicken livers,
  trimmed and finely
  chopped

200g/8oz minced/ground
  pork

450g/1lb/2½ cups basmati or
  other long-grain white rice,
  rinsed and drained

½ tsp ground cumin

½ tsp paprika

1 tsp ground coriander

1 tsp dried or fresh oregano

750ml/26fl oz/3¼ cups
  chicken stock

1 small bunch of coriander/
  cilantro, chopped
  (optional)

Heat the oil in a large heavy-based wok. Add the onions and garlic and fry over a medium-high heat until they are golden brown. Add the celery, chilli and peppers and fry for a further minute until they are soft.

Now add the chopped livers and turn up the heat. You want them to turn brown and caramelize. Be careful not to burn them but they should cook quite briskly.

Once brown, add the pork and cook over a medium heat until the meat is sealed. Keep breaking up the clumps. It is important that the texture of the meat matches that of the rice.

Now add the rice, the dried spices and oregano. Pour in the stock and bring the dish to a gentle boil over a medium-high heat, then turn the heat down to medium-low and simmer for 15–20 minutes, uncovered, until the rice is tender and the stock has almost all been absorbed.

Now fit on a tight lid, switch off the heat and leave the pan for 10 minutes.

It is now ready to serve. Sprinkle over the chopper coriander/cilantro – I love the perfumed lift it gives to the dish.

Going up to Cajun country

Rice proved to be a valuable commodity in early Cajun country. With an abundance of water and a hot, humid climate, rice could be grown practically anywhere in the region and grew wild in some areas. So it became the predominant starch, easy to grow, store and prepare.

Cajun cuisine is 'country cooking' in Louisiana. A truly Cajun meal is usually tripartite. One pot is dedicated to the main dish, one pot is dedicated to steamed rice and a third will contain the vegetable element.

With no access to modern-day luxuries like refrigerators, early Cajuns learned to make use of every part of a slaughtered animal. When a pig is butchered the event is called a *boucherie*. *Boudin*, a type of Cajun sausage that consists of pork meat, rice and seasoning stuffed into a casing, also commonly contains pig liver for a little extra flavour. And it is the liver that gives dirty rice its hardcore look and its deep flavour. I use chicken liver in this recipe as it is easy to buy and I find it to be sweeter and more chocolatey than pig livers. Pig livers taste fattier and pinker, if that makes sense. We want brown to the eye and brown to the taste in this dish.

Dirty rice is a big name on the Cajun rice scene. Cajun chefs consider pepper, onion and celery to be the holy trinity of both Cajun and Creole cuisines – and garlic is the pope! These ingredients are chopped and added to the cooking process rather like the *mirepoix* method in classical French cuisine – Cajun finishing touches reach for parsley and freshly ground black pepper.

Serves: 4
Prep: 15 minutes
Cook: 1 hour

Pollo arroz

This is a Spanish/Latin American classic and, by Jove, they know how to wield smoked paprika and chicken better than anyone in the world!

1 whole chicken, cut into
    8 pieces
1 tbsp olive oil
2 small onions, chopped
4 garlic cloves, crushed
1 red pepper, deseeded and
    cut into long thick strips
2 tsp sweet smoked paprika
240g/8¾oz/1¼ cups
    long-grain white rice,
    rinsed and drained
200ml/7fl oz/scant 1 cup dry
    white wine
200g/7oz can chopped
    tomatoes
300ml/10½fl oz/1¼ cups
    chicken stock
½ tsp saffron strands
2 preserved lemons,
    quartered
2 small bay leaves
100g/3½oz/¾ cup frozen
    peas, defrosted
10 pitted green olives, halved
salt and freshly ground black
    pepper

Season the chicken pieces with salt and pepper. Heat the oil in a heavy-based pan and once it reaches a high heat, add the pieces of chicken, turning them briskly to ensure the chicken is browned on all sides. Remove the chicken from the pan and leave to one side.

Add the onions, garlic and pepper to the pan and cook over a medium heat until the onions become soft and translucent.

Add the smoked paprika and rice and stir-fry over a medium heat for a minute until all the grains are covered and smell sweetly smoked.

Add the wine and increase the heat to a medium-high. Once the wine boils, add the tomatoes, chicken stock, saffron, preserved lemons and bay leaves.

Turn the heat down to low and return the chicken pieces and any juices to the pan, covering the chicken pieces in the rice mix. Cover the pan and simmer gently until the chicken is cooked through and most of the liquid has been absorbed by the rice. This usually takes around 20–25 minutes.

Remove from the heat and stir in the peas and olives. Season with salt and pepper to taste. Cover tightly and leave the dish to stand for 15 minutes. Serve hot.

Belly bonnet biryani

I call this a biryani but it's more like a rice cassoulet. This is the stuff of a swift supper with a crisp salad, not an elaborate affair. Scotch bonnet is the headline ingredient because it has such an incredible flavour. I make this dish in a pressure cooker, which takes minutes and gives you that buttery, smoked Scotch bonnet high if you pop them in for the last 10 minutes. The earlier you add the Scotch bonnets, the milder the dish. Drop them in later and you will get more heat but accompanied by that addictive smoky come-hither.

1 tbsp pine nuts

2 tbsp sunflower oil

5cm/2in piece of fresh root ginger, peeled and grated

2 garlic cloves, crushed

2 green cardamom pods, lightly crushed

3 whole cloves

200g/7oz belly pork, cut into 2.5cm/1in cubes

½ tsp turmeric

1 tbsp butter

3 onions, thinly sliced

1 green finger chilli, deseeded and chopped

2 tsp garam masala

2 star anise

1 tsp ground cumin

1 tsp brown sugar

1 tsp ground coriander

200g/7oz/1¼ cups white basmati rice, rinsed and drained

200g/7oz can chopped tomatoes

1 orange Scotch bonnet, deseeded and finely chopped

1 tbsp chopped coriander/cilantro leaves

salt

Put the pine nuts in a dry frying pan over a medium-high heat and toast until brown. Remove and leave to one side.

Heat 1 tablespoon oil in a heavy-based saucepan (or, better still, in a pressure cooker) and add the ginger, garlic, cardamom pods and cloves and a pinch of salt. Fry over a medium-high heat for around 1 minute. Add the belly pork pieces and turmeric and continue to fry until the meat begins to brown.

Add about 120ml/4fl oz/½ cup cold water and bring to the boil. Turn the heat down to medium-low, cover the pan and leave to simmer for 30–40 minutes until the meat is tender. Top up with water from time to time just to ensure the meat stays moist and there are liquids to simmer. Once the meat is soft, remove the pan from the heat. If you are using a saucepan, it will take 30 minutes but in a pressure cooker, this process takes around 10–15 minutes.

Heat the remaining oil with the butter in a large heavy-based pan and fry the onions for about 10 minutes until golden brown. Lift out one-third of the onions, using a slotted spoon, and drain on paper towels, to reserve for a finishing garnish.

Now add the green chilli, garam masala, star anise, ground cumin, brown sugar and ground coriander and fry for 1 minute. Stir in the basmati rice and fry over a medium heat for 2 minutes. Add the tomatoes and chopped Scotch bonnet and continue to fry for 2–3 minutes.

Now transfer the pan of cooked pork belly and the juices and spices to the large pan and combine carefully. Add 480ml/16fl oz/2 cups cold water, bring the dish to the boil over a high heat, then turn down the heat to low and leave to simmer for 20–25 minutes until the rice has absorbed almost all the water. Now carefully stir in the chopped coriander/cilantro. Cover, remove from the heat and leave for 10–15 minutes.

Turn the biryani out on a plate and sprinkle with the reserved browned onions and pine nuts to serve.

Tomato pork bombs

Serves: 4
Prep: 30 minutes
Cook: 40 minutes

This is a very precious dish to me as it is one of my mother-in-law's signature dishes – the most delicious, sweet meaty dumplings nestling in a rich, velvety, wrap-you-in-a-blanket tomato sauce. A Hungarian tomato sauce is quite unlike its Italian cousins. The liquid comes from the stock the meat was cooked in, blended with tomato purée/paste, or sometimes from fresh, puréed tomatoes. Hungarians serve it with boiled potatoes but I think the rich meatballs and soft, soupy sauce are better when they stand alone.

50g/1¾oz/heaped ¼ cup white basmati rice, rinsed and drained

2 tbsp sunflower oil, plus extra for oiling

2 small onions, chopped

450g/1lb minced/ground pork

1 egg, lightly beaten

¼ tsp dried marjoram

1 tbsp chopped parsley leaves

1 tsp paprika

2½ tsp salt

¼ tsp freshly ground black pepper

THE TOMATO SAUCE

2 tbsp butter, softened

1½ tbsp plain/all-purpose flour

1 tbsp cornflour/cornstarch

6 tbsp tomato purée/paste

2 tbsp sugar

½ tsp salt

2 tbsp red wine vinegar

Put the rice and 120 ml/4fl oz/½ cup water in a saucepan over a medium-high heat and bring to the boil. Turn the heat down to low and simmer for 5 minutes until the grains just begin to soften so that they can be crushed easily between the fingers. Drain and rinse with cold water to stop the cooking process.

Heat the oil in a frying pan and sauté the onions over a medium heat for about 5 minutes until soft.

Mix the minced/ground pork, rice, onions, egg, marjoram, parsley, paprika, ½ teaspoon of the salt and the black pepper in a large mixing bowl.

Fill a large saucepan with water and add 2 teaspoons of salt to the water. Bring to the boil.

With oiled hands, form meatballs about 4cm/1½in in diameter. Drop the balls into the vigorously boiling water and cook for 8–10 minutes until the balls become firm. Remove carefully and put on a tray, reserving the cooking liquid.

Meanwhile, to make the sauce, melt the butter in a saucepan over a low heat. Sprinkle the flour over the butter, stir and cook until the mixture foams up. Do not let it brown. Blend the cornflour/cornstarch to a paste with 2 tablespoons water. Stir the tomato purée/paste and 950ml/32fl oz/4 cups of the water in which the meatballs were cooked into the sauce and bring to the boil, stirring continuously. As it comes to the boil, stir in the cornflour/cornstarch paste until the sauce thickens.

Stir in the sugar, salt and the red wine vinegar. Taste and adjust the seasoning with salt and pepper, if needed. Add more sugar or vinegar to suit your taste. You are looking for a sweet, tangy tomato base.

Now carefully transfer the meatballs to the tomato sauce. Loosen with a touch of water to ensure that the meatballs are covered with the tomato sauce. Simmer gently for 15 minutes until the meatballs are cooked through. Serve straight away.

Ants climbing trees

Serves: 4
Prep: 25 minutes, plus soaking
Cook: 25 minutes

I cook this at least once a week. If I have minced/ground meat in the refrigerator, I'm usually inclined to head East just before I get to spaghetti bolognaise and this is frequently where I end up, a fragrant, umami minced/ground meat and noodle tangle, the look of which gives the dish its evocative name. I usually throw in some chopped green beans to cook with the meat if I have them in. This ticks the 'health' box which, for me, appears woefully lower in priority than the one labelled 'flavour'. For extra citrus, mind-numbing punch, add a teaspoon of whole Szechuan peppercorns into the meat as it fries.

125g/4½oz minced/ground pork
½ tsp light soy sauce
½ tsp Shaoxing rice wine
½ tsp toasted sesame oil
125g/4½oz fine rice noodles
1 tbsp sunflower oil
1 garlic clove, finely chopped
2.5cm/1in piece of fresh root ginger, peeled and finely chopped
2 spring onions/scallions, finely chopped, green parts reserved and sliced
1 tsp chilli bean paste
1 tbsp chopped coriander/cilantro leaves

THE SHAOXING WINE SAUCE
1 tbsp light soy sauce
1 tbsp Shaoxing rice wine
½ tsp salt
½ tsp sugar
½ tsp toasted sesame oil
240ml/8fl oz/1 cup chicken stock

Mix the pork with the soy sauce, rice wine and sesame oil. Soak the noodles in hot water for 10 minutes until limp, then drain

Heat a wok over a high heat and add the oil. Add the garlic and ginger and fry for 10 seconds. Add the pork and stir-fry, mashing and separating it. It needs to brown and this should take around 10 minutes. Now add the spring onions/scallions and chilli paste and stir-fry for a few seconds.

Meanwhile, make the sauce by combining all the sauce ingredients. Now pour the sauce into the meat and toss the ingredients together well.

Add the noodles to the meat sauce mix and return the dish to a medium-high heat. It needs to boil. Reduce the heat to low and cook for a further 5 minutes until the noodles become soft and infused with flavour. Most of the liquid will need to evaporate.

Serve sprinkled with the sliced spring onion/scallion greens and coriander/cilantro leaves.

Red rice rendang

The Indonesian palette of flavours is intriguingly unique. Lemongrass, galangal and kaffir lime leaves are hugely fragrant and give the beef a brave feminine dimension. It is so important that the beef becomes tender and utterly penetrable to these iconic spicings.

50g/1¾oz/1 cup coconut flakes

2 lemongrass stalks, hard outer layers removed

2 small onions, chopped

3 garlic cloves, chopped

6cm/2½in piece of fresh root ginger, peeled and grated

1 tbsp chopped fresh galangal, or paste

4–6 red chillies, deseeded and roughly chopped

1 tsp turmeric

2 tbsp oil

4 cardamom pods, lightly crushed

1 cinnamon stick

650g/1lb 7oz braising steak, diced into 3cm/1¼in cubes

400ml/14fl oz/1⅔ cups coconut milk

4 kaffir lime leaves

grated zest and juice of 1 lime

190g/6¾oz/1 cup red rice, preferably Bhutanese, soaked overnight, then drained

salt

2 shallots, finely sliced and deep fried

2 tbsp chopped coriander/cilantro leaves

First, make the Rendang paste. Toast the coconut flakes in a dry frying pan until browned, then remove them from the heat. Roughly chop 1 lemongrass stalk. Blitz together the toasted coconut, onions, ginger, galangal, chopped lemongrass, garlic, chillies and turmeric to a smooth paste.

Now heat a wok and add the oil. Fry the spice paste over a high heat for about 3–5 minutes. Add the cardamom and cinnamon stick. Cook for a minute over a medium heat. Now add the beef and fry it over a medium-high heat until the pieces are browned, stirring constantly.

Add the coconut milk, kaffir lime leaves and lime zest and juice and simmer very gently so that the pan is barely bubbling. Bruise the remaining lemongrass and add it to the pan. Season with salt and partially cover. Cook over a low heat for 1 hour. The meat needs to be very tender but not disintegrated. Discard the lemongrass stalk.

Add the rice and raise the heat a little to medium-low. Simmer for a further 20–25 minutes or until the rice is cooked through. Switch off the heat and put a lid on the pan. Leave to rest and for the flavours to combine for 15 minutes before serving.

To serve, transfer to a large dish, and sprinkle with the deep-fried shallots and the coriander/cilantro.

Layered leaf lasagne

Serves: 4
Prep: 35 minutes
Cook: 1 hour
15 minutes

This is a genius Hungarian classic. It's a fantastically quirky concept to us in Western Europe but in Budapest, it's as common as goulash. It is also a great way to use up leftover rice. I like to use lamb but this works brilliantly with any minced/ground meat or even soy, if you are so inclined.

400ml/14fl oz/1⅔ cups
   sour cream
1 egg
1 Savoy cabbage, trimmed
   and cored
3 tbsp sunflower oil, plus
   extra for greasing
115g/4oz smoked bacon,
   finely diced
1 tsp paprika
2 onions, finely chopped
2 garlic cloves, crushed
600g/1lb 5oz minced/
   ground lamb
¼ tsp dried marjoram
1 tbsp plain/all-purpose flour
300ml/10½fl oz/1¼ cups
   vegetable stock
55g/2oz/scant ⅔ cup
   long-grain white rice,
   rinsed and drained
200g/7oz/2½ cups golden
   breadcrumbs
salt and freshly ground black
   pepper

Beat the sour cream and egg in a mixing bowl. Leave to one side.

Separate the cabbage leaves, ensuring they come off in one piece as these will form your layers of 'leaf lasagne'. Blanch these leaves in a large pan of boiling salted water, then drain. They should be limp and pliable.

Heat the oil in a wide saucepan and add the bacon. Once it has browned and rendered its fat, add the paprika, onions and garlic. Cook over a medium heat until the onions begin to turn brown. Add the minced/ground lamb and the marjoram and fry over a medium heat for 10–15 minutes until the lamb is browned. Stir in the flour and cook for 1 minute. Now add the stock, bring to the boil, then simmer for 5 minutes. Season with salt and pepper to taste.

Bring the rice and 240ml/8fl oz/1 cup water to the boil over a medium-high heat in a separate saucepan. Reduce the heat to medium and simmer for 10 minutes. Drain and rinse with cold water. Leave to one side.

Preheat the oven to 180°C/350°F/Gas 4. Grease a high-sided baking dish about 25cm/10in across.

Gently mix the cooked rice into the pan of cooked lamb.

Lay one-third of the cabbage leaves, the smallest ones, in a circle on the bottom of the dish. Spread one-third of the meat filling on top. You are aiming for a meat layer of around 2cm/¾in deep.

Next, spoon over about one-third of the sour cream mixture, enough to cover the meat layer. It will begin to seep through but do not worry. Sprinkle some of the golden breadcrumbs over the top.

Now repeat the procedure, covering this layer with the medium-size leaves, and ensuring that you finish with a layer of cabbage covered with sour cream, then finally breadcrumbs.

Bake for about 35 minutes or until the top is golden and bubbling, then leave to rest for around 15 minutes. Serve hot, cut into wedges.

Total tagine

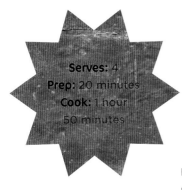

Ultimately comforting, this is a great one-pot wonder. Long-cooked lamb releases the most wonderful juices into this dish. The heady notes of the cumin, cinnamon, ginger and cardamom are absorbed into the tender flesh and only good can come of this.

2 tbsp sunflower oil

1 large onion, chopped

2cm/¾in piece of fresh root ginger, peeled and grated

2 garlic cloves

1½ tsp ground cumin

1 tsp turmeric

¼ tsp chilli powder

2 green cardamom pods

2 star anise

1 tsp ground coriander

1 cinnamon stick

100g/3½oz/⅔ cup dried apricots

200g/7oz can chopped tomatoes

750g/1lb 10oz lamb shoulder, cut into 4cm/1½in cubes

1 tbsp muscovado/soft brown sugar

90g/3¼oz/scant ½ cup white basmati rice, rinsed and drained

100g/3½oz/¾ cup pitted prunes

1 handful of coriander/ cilantro leaves, chopped

salt and freshly ground black pepper

Heat the oil in a large saucepan and add the onion, ginger and garlic. Fry until they become golden brown. Add the cumin, turmeric, chilli powder, cardamom, star anise, ground coriander, cinnamon and apricots. Fry for 5 minutes over a medium heat to encourage the spices to release their aromas. Add the tomatoes and fry for a further 5 minutes.

Turn up the heat to medium-high, add the meat and fry on all sides until it is browned. Cover with 1 litre/35fl oz/4⅓ cups water, add the sugar and season with salt and pepper. Bring to the boil, then turn the heat down to low and simmer, partially covered, for 1 hour.

Stir in the rice and prunes and continue to cook for 25–30 minutes until the rice has become tender.

Transfer to a large serving plate and scatter with the coriander/cilantro to serve.

Serves: 4
Prep: 30 minutes, plus marinating
Cook: 50 minutes

Lebanese rose petal rice

The succulent charred lamb and woody aromatic spices give a deep earthy foundation to this well-loved Lebanese home favourite, as much as the saffron and the rose petals give it an elegant sophisticated edge. It is delicious served with cooling minted yogurt.

300g/10½oz boned leg of lamb, cut into cubes

30g/1oz/¼ cup dried apricots, roughly chopped

½ tsp saffron strands

800ml/28fl oz/3½ cups vegetable stock

½ tsp sea salt

25g/1oz/scant ¼ cup pine nuts

300g/10½oz/1⅔ cups white basmati rice, rinsed and drained

1 tbsp salted butter

1 tbsp sunflower oil

4 green cardamom pods

2 cinnamon sticks

grated zest of 1 lemon

2 tbsp dried rose petals

1 tablespoon chopped pistachios

a few fresh rose petals

a few small mint leaves

seeds of ½ pomegranate

yogurt and chopped mint dip

THE MARINADE

200g/7oz/heaped ¾ cup yogurt

2 tsp ground cumin

2 tsp garlic purée

2 tsp ginger paste

juice of ½ lemon

Combine all the marinade ingredients in a non-metallic bowl. Add the lamb and leave to marinate for least 1 hour.

When you are ready to cook, preheat the grill/broiler to high. Lift the lamb pieces out of the marinade and grill/broil them until they just begin to char. Leave to one side.

Meanwhile, soak the chopped apricots and the saffron in the stock with the salt added. Toast the pine nuts in a dry frying pan until they begin to brown.

Heat the butter and oil in a large heavy-based pan with a tightly fitting lid. Add the cardamom pods and the cinnamon sticks and fry gently for 1 minute. Now turn up the heat and add the rice, tossing the grains in the perfumed butter.

Add the stock, with the apricots and saffron, and the lemon zest. Allow the dish to bubble over a medium-low heat for about 8–10 minutes until half of the liquid has been absorbed.

Now add the lamb pieces and the dried rose petals. Cook, uncovered, over a medium-low heat until almost all the water has been absorbed. Clamp a lid on the pan, switch off the heat and leave the pan for 15 minutes without disturbing it.

After 15 minutes, remove the lid and transfer the cooked rice dish to a large serving plate. Toss in the pine nuts and the pistachios. Strew the finished dish with the fresh rose petals, the mint leaves and adorn with the pomegranate seeds. Serve with a cooling yogurt and chopped mint dip.

Gin & tonic coriander salmon

Juniper, gin and salmon. There is nothing new under the sun, I realise that, but the addition of the tonic to this dish may put the theory to the test. I tried it in a moment of reckless adventure. Once cooked, the tonic water added a shrill, sweet edge to the salmon that I found most pleasing. The title reads like a contrived 1970's toe curler but I urge you, open your mind and give it a whirl.

½ tbsp olive oil

1 garlic clove, crushed

2 juniper berries, crushed

grated zest and juice of 1½ limes

2 tsp ground coriander

1 tsp chopped coriander/ cilantro leaves, plus extra to serve

3 tbsp gin

5 tbsp tonic water

4 x 125g/4½oz salmon fillets

200g/7oz/heaped 1 cup white basmati rice, rinsed and drained

1 lime, cut into wedges

salt and freshly ground black pepper

Put the oil, garlic, juniper berries, lime zest and juice, ground coriander, coriander/cilantro leaves and gin and tonic in a mixing bowl and season with salt and pepper. Put the salmon fillet, flesh-side down, in the mixture, cover and refrigerate for at least 2 hours.

Preheat the oven to 200°C/400°F/Gas 6.

Select a shallow heatproof casserole dish and create a foil tent into which you can fit the four salmon fillets. Bear in mind there should be enough foil to tent over the fish and to seal.

Transfer the fish with the juices into the foil tent. Bring the foil sides up and seal the fish into a parcel. Put the casserole dish in the oven and bake for 15–20 minutes.

Meanwhile, put the rice and 480ml/16fl oz/2 cups water in a heavy-based saucepan and bring to the boil over a high heat. Reduce the heat to medium and simmer for about 10 minutes until the rice has absorbed almost all the water. Clamp a lid on the pan, remove from the heat and leave for 10 minutes.

Remove the foil tent from the oven and open it up. Carefully spoon the cooked basmati rice around the sides of the fish into the juices. Sprinkle with a few coriander/cilantro leaves, grind a little black pepper over the top and dot with lime wedges to serve.

Turkish stuffed mussels

A molluscian Fisher-Price activity centre of a dish to construct and to eat ... but boy is it worth it! It shames me that in Turkey these works of dark, gleaming, fragrant art are common waterfront 'street food'. It puts our pasty in a paper bag to shame. The Turkish enjoy this dish served cold and brush the shells with a little oil to give them a dark, beckoning glint.

2 tbsp raisins

125g/4½oz/⅔ cup risotto or other short-grain white rice, rinsed and drained

28 large large mussels, cleaned and bearded

2 tbsp olive oil

3 tbsp pine nuts

1 banana shallot, finely diced

1 small garlic clove, crushed

a small pinch of freshly grated nutmeg

½ tsp ground cinnamon

½ tsp allspice

1 tsp soft brown sugar

½ tsp tomato purée/paste

1 tsp salt

1 tsp finely chopped mint leaves

1 tsp finely chopped dill

freshly ground black pepper

1 lemon, cut into wedges

Soak the raisins in a little warm water for 10–15 minutes, then drain. Put the rice in a large bowl, cover with cold water and leave to soak for 10 minutes. Drain and leave to one side. Soak the cleaned mussels in a large bowl of warm water for about 10 minutes.

Heat the oil in a heavy-based saucepan and fry the pine nuts over a medium heat until brown. Add the shallot, garlic, spices and sugar and cook over a medium-low heat for 5 minutes. Stir in the drained rice, tomato purée/paste and raisins. Cook for 2 minutes, mixing well.

Season with the salt and pepper, add 320ml/11fl oz/1⅓ cups water and bring to the boil. Turn the heat down and cover with a tight-fitting lid. Cook for 15 minutes, or until the liquid has been absorbed. Transfer the rice to a shallow bowl, stir in the chopped mint and dill and leave to cool.

To prepare the mussels, use a small, sharp knife and work over a large bowl to catch and reserve the juices. Clasp each mussel by its thinner end, with the sharper edge facing outwards. Insert the knife between the two shells near the rounded top and cut through where the mussel is attached. Carefully prise the shells open just a little, keeping the mussels in the shells. Discard any that smell unpleasant or are discoloured or sticky and any that do not have a tightly closed shell. If in doubt, discard the mussel.

Now take a teaspoon and gently ease a generous amount of rice into each mussel. Squeeze the shells shut and wipe away the excess filling. Stack the mussels in a colander and cover with damp baking parchment. Put a plate on top to restrict the mussels from opening too wide as they cook.

Strain the reserved mussel juice into a measuring jug and add enough water to make it up to about 500ml/17fl oz/generous 2 cups. Empty this into a large, heavy-based saucepan. Put the colander full of mussels in the pan. Cover, bring to the boil, then simmer for 20 minutes.

Remove from the heat and let the mussels cool in the pan. Serve at room temperature or refrigerate for at least 1 hour and serve cold. To serve, stack the mussels on a serving plate. Break off the top shell, squeeze on a little lemon juice, then use the loose shell to scoop out the contents.

Paella rice

Paella rice is not actually a distinct variety of rice grain but simply a broad description of rice grains that work well in paella. Varieties include Bahia, Balilla, Senia and Bomba.

What is required of paella rice is that the grains adhere to each other and absorb a good amount of liquid. What is not required is the creation of a creamy sauce. That is what is demanded from a risotto rice and herein lies the big difference between the two.

Any short-grain rice is fine for the domestic kitchen. There are some that promise the most extraordinary results, super-absorbent weapon-like grains like the Spanish varieties noted above. Go for them if you can afford to. In my humble view, risotto and sushi rice make just about acceptable substitutes.

The debate, however, rages on. Short grain or long grain? To stir or not to stir? The general consensus is that short grain is best as it absorbs liquid and then does not dry out in the wide, drying paella pan. This has to make sense, surely. And do not stir; the liquid needs to cook off briskly because you do not want a creamy finish – this isn't a risotto! What you are looking for is a softness but with spine. The deeper brown, crisp, burnt layer at the bottom has a name: socarrat. It is the part to fight for. Feign selfless grace, serve your guests first and then hack away with an 'oh it's fine, I don't mind the burnt bits'.

How to cook paella rice

* Use 1 cup of rice to just under 2 cups of liquid (190g/6¾oz rice to 450ml/15fl oz water).

* Put the rice in a colander and rinse under cold running water until the water runs clear. Leave to drain.

* Put the rice in a saucepan and add the cooking liquid (wine, stock or water). Bring to the boil, then simmer gently for about 35 minutes, uncovered, until the liquid has been absorbed and the rice is moist and juicy.

* Cover tightly, remove from the heat and leave to stand for 10 minutes.

Easy peasy paella

A sunshine dish whatever the budget. In my view, it is the garnishing prawns/shrimp, gowned in full shelled splendour, that give this dish its fur-coat moment. The flavour legwork is done below, in folds of oozing golden rice, by humble, inexpensive fish, coaxed to impress by the odd clever ingredient. I use turmeric to coat the fish – it gives it an earthy, golden edge that carries beautifully into the paella. I find the turmeric a more substantial addition than the expensive and diaphanous saffron.

4 tomatoes

300g/10½oz any white fish fillets, skinned and cut into chunks

1 heaped tsp turmeric

1 tsp salt

4 tbsp olive oil

1 onion, chopped

3 garlic cloves, finely chopped

1 red pepper, deseeded and sliced

225g/8oz/scant 1¼ cups paella or risotto rice, rinsed and drained

450ml/15fl oz/scant 2 cups fish stock

150ml/5fl oz/scant ⅔ cup white wine

115g/4oz peeled prawns/shrimp

75g/2½oz/⅔ cup frozen peas

8 mussels, scrubbed and bearded

4 large cooked prawns/shrimp, shell and heads on

1 lemon, cut into 4 wedges

1 tbsp chopped parsley leaves

salt and freshly ground black pepper

Score a cross on the top of each tomato, then plunge into a bowl of boiling water, then a bowl of cold water. Leave until cool enough to handle, then peel off the skin and chop the flesh.

Toss the fish fillets in the turmeric and salt.

Heat half the oil in a large frying pan or paella pan and add the fish. Stir-fry for 2 minutes over a high heat, then remove the fish from the pan and leave to one aside.

Add the rest of the oil to the pan, then add the onion and garlic and fry until transparent. Add the pepper and fry until soft. Stir in the tomatoes and fry for a couple of minutes.

Now add the rice and stir for 2 minutes. Pour in the fish stock, the white wine and the cooked turmeric fish with its juices. Add the peeled prawns/shrimp.

Submerge the mussels into the bubbling rice and cover. Cook over a gentle heat for about 30 minutes. Add the peas and cook for a further 5 minutes. The stock needs to be absorbed and the rice moist and juicy. Discard any mussels that do not open.

Arrange the mussels and whole prawns/shrimp dramatically on top and heat through for 1 minute, then remove the pan from the heat, cover and allow the paella to stand for at least 10 minutes. Sprinkle with the chopped parsley to serve.

Salmon & saffron risotto

Serves: 4
Prep: 10 minutes
Cook: 30 minutes

I really struggled with this risotto for a long time. I loved the elegant salmon-saffron combination but felt that it was almost too delicate and diaphanous. It was the addition of the Parmesan that gave the dish a wonderfully creamy tang and length of flavour.

75g/2½oz/5 tbsp butter

1 onion, finely chopped

275g/10oz/scant 1½ cups risotto rice, rinsed and drained

1.2 litres/40fl oz/5 cups hot chicken stock

8 saffron strands, left to steep for 10 minutes in a small bowl of hot water

80g/2¾oz/heaped 1 cup freshly grated Parmesan cheese

350g/12oz salmon fillet, finely sliced

salt and freshly ground black pepper

Heat half the butter in a saucepan and fry the onion until softened. Add the rice and stir for about 4 minutes. Add the stock, ladle by ladle, stirring over a low heat until all the water is absorbed. Add the saffron and its soaking water. It should take around 20 minutes for all the water to be absorbed and for the risotto to be creamy and moist.

Now stir in the remaining butter and the Parmesan. As soon as this is melted into the risotto, add the salmon slices. Stir very gently and cook for 2 more minutes until the fish is just cooked through.

Remove from the heat immediately and season with salt and pepper to taste. Serve hot with a twist of sharpening black pepper on top.

Just jambalaya

For a while back there in the early 90s, thoughts of this dish were hijacked by a certain choking scene in the film *Mrs Doubtfire*. Most unfair, as this Cajun-inspired and sweetly meaty dish can be all things to all people. It has huge amounts of flavour and texture. I give you here two options. The lightweight option – lightweight in terms of emotions not cholesterol – involves lots of peeled prawns/shrimp and, in this way, becomes an incidental pleasure. Then there is the full-on option – centre-stage, drag-queen prawns/shrimp, complete with head and shell. Judge your diners carefully. Have your Heimlich handy.

350g/12oz tomatoes or canned chopped tomatoes

2 tbsp butter

750g/1lb 10oz chicken drumsticks and thighs on the bone

225g/8oz smoked pancetta, as lean as you can find it

30g/1oz/scant ¼ cup plain/all-purpose flour

2 small onions, diced

1 green pepper, deseeded and diced

1 large garlic clove, crushed

1 tsp chopped thyme leaves or ½ tsp dried thyme

225g/8oz/1¼ cups long-grain white rice, rinsed and drained

16 prawns/shrimp, peeled and deveined or

12 medium/large prawns/shrimp, shell and head on

1 tsp Tabasco sauce

1½ tbsp chopped flat-leaf parsley leaves

salt and freshly ground black pepper

If using fresh tomatoes, score a cross on the top of each tomato, then plunge into a bowl of boiling water, then a bowl of cold water. Leave until cool enough to handle, then peel off the skin and chop the flesh.

Heat a large heavy-based frying pan and drop in the butter. Once melted, turn up to a medium-high heat and batch-fry the chicken pieces. They should just be browned all over. This should take 2–3 minutes on each side. Remove from the pan with a slotted spoon and leave to one side.

Repeat this with the pancetta and set that aside.

Turn the heat down to low and toss the flour into the fat in the pan. Stir until the flour and fat turn golden brown. Return the chicken and pancetta to the pan. Now add the onions, pepper, tomatoes, garlic and thyme. Cook for 10 minutes, stirring frequently to prevent sticking.

Stir in the rice and pour on 600ml/20fl oz/2½ cups water. Season with salt and pepper. Simmer gently over a medium heat until the rice is tender and almost all the liquid has been absorbed. This should take about 20–30 minutes.

Toss in the prawns/shrimp and the Tabasco sauce. Stir in gently and turn down the heat to low and cook for a further 5 minutes, or until all the liquid has been absorbed.

Now put a tightly fitting lid on the pan and switch off the heat. Allow the rice to sit for 10 minutes.

Serve hot, sprinkled with the chopped flat-leaf parsley for that fresh edge and pretty finish.

Serves: 4
Prep: 25 minutes
Cook: 1 hour
15 minutes

Gutsy prawn gumbo

The guts of New Orleans. Green chillies for green fresh heat, Scotch bonnet for peppery smoked flavour, smoked paprika to give legs to the opening sprint of the chorizo.

100g/3½oz chorizo, peeled and diced

100g/3½oz okra, chopped into 5mm/¼in discs

4 tbsp sunflower oil

2 onions, finely chopped

3 garlic cloves, crushed

2 green chillies, deseeded and finely chopped (optional)

1 green pepper, deseeded and chopped

3 tbsp plain/all-purpose flour

400g/14oz can chopped tomatoes

1 litre/35fl oz/4⅓ cups chicken stock, plus extra if needed

2 tbsp chopped parsley leaves, plus extra to serve

1 tsp dried thyme

1 bay leaf

½ small orange Scotch bonnet chilli, deseeded and finely chopped (optional)

1 tsp sweet smoked paprika

3 skinless, boneless chicken thighs, cut into 2cm/¾in cubes

180g/6¼oz/1 cup white basmati rice, rinsed and drained

250g/9oz peeled large raw prawns/shrimp

salt and freshly ground black pepper

Fry the chorizo in a heavy-based saucepan over a medium heat until the fat has rendered out and the pieces become browned and slightly crisped. Use a slotted spoon to remove the pieces and set them aside, leaving the chorizo oil in the pan.

Add the okra pieces to the pan and fry over a medium-high heat until they become crisp and lose their slime. This takes 5–8 minutes. Remove and leave to one side.

Now add ½ tablespoon sunflower oil to the pan and add the onions, garlic, green chillies and pepper and fry over a medium-high heat for 5 minutes. Remove the vegetables and set them aside.

Add the rest of the oil to the pan and sprinkle in the flour. Stir continuously and cook for 5 minutes over a low heat until the flour is browned.

Stir in the tomatoes, stock, parsley, thyme, bay leaf, Scotch bonnet and smoked paprika and bring to the boil. Reduce the heat to low and simmer for 30 minutes.

Add the chicken and rice to the pan with the fried vegetables, except the okra. Bring to the boil, then reduce the heat and simmer for 15 minutes, or until the rice is soft and the chicken cooked through. If at any point you feel the dish is too dry, add a little more stock to keep the rice moist.

Season with salt and pepper to taste and add the prawns/shrimp and chorizo, then simmer for a further 5 minutes until the prawns/shrimp are cooked through. At the last minute, add the crisp okra discs and stir in carefully. Sprinkle with parsley and serve hot.

Jollof rice

This is the ultimate West African party dish. It is made in huge pans, often with whole chickens. The colour is a festive red and the taste is sweet, savoury, punchy with the zing of the peppers, and yet has a quickening tang that makes the dish a meal in itself. It is all things to all party goers.

Serves: 4
Prep: 15 minutes
Cook: 45 minutes

2 tbsp sunflower oil

2 tbsp butter

1 onion, chopped

2.5cm/1in piece of fresh root
  ginger, peeled and grated

2 garlic cloves, crushed

1 large red pepper, deseeded
  and diced

400g/14oz can chopped
  tomatoes

½ Scotch bonnet, deseeded
  (optional)

1 tbsp tomato purée/paste

1 tbsp thyme leaves or
  1 tsp dried thyme

½ tsp sweet smoked paprika

1 tsp paprika

1 heaped tsp ground cumin

2 tbsp dried shrimp

1 tsp soft brown sugar

350g/12oz/scant 2 cups
  white basmati rice, rinsed
  and drained

750ml/26fl oz/generous
  3 cups chicken stock

freshly snipped chives

salt

Heat the oil and butter in a deep heavy-based saucepan. Add the onion, ginger, garlic and red pepper and fry over a medium heat until the onion begins to become brown and sweet.

Add the tomatoes, Scotch bonnet, tomato purée/paste, thyme, both the paprikas, the ground cumin, dried shrimp and sugar and season with salt to taste. Simmer this mixture over a medium-low heat for around 8 minutes. The oils in the mixture should begin to stain red and sit as a veneer on top of the tomato sauce.

With a hand blender or a conventional blender, blend the mixture to a smooth paste, then return it to the pan if necessary.

Stir in the rice and continue to stir for about 3 minutes over a medium-low heat. Now slowly pour in the stock and simmer over a low heat for about 20 minutes. Stir occasionally during the early stages of cooking but never once the rice begins to form a more solid mass. If the rice begins to look very dry, add a little extra water. Once all the liquid has been absorbed, put a tightly fitting lid over the rice and switch off the heat. Leave the pan for 10 minutes.

Remove the lid, sprinkle with the snipped chives and serve either on its own or as sweet, heat-tinged accompaniment to chicken and fish dishes.

Unctuous one-pot creations

Invented in the empire of Jollof by the Wolof peoples of West Africa, this dish is also known as *benachin,* which translates as 'one pot'. Most West African nations have a variation of it. At its core is the one-pot method of unctuous rice creation where tomato is added to seep right into the heart of the rice grain and so sweeten and brighten it. Some use coconut milk as the liquid and some use Rooibos or red bush tea. Tomato purée/paste, onions, salt and hot peppers are the general direction that the various West African nations head in. After that, the kind of meat, veg and spices that are lobbed in are entirely down to how the chef feels on the day, or rather what is seasonal and what he has to hand. This kind of liberal history to the dish means you can experiment with whatever you fancy, once you have cracked the basics of Jollof.

I remember being invited for my first Jollof rice lunch by a good Nigerian pal of mine. It was served in a huge steel catering-event-sized pan. I recall prodding around subtly for meat, preferably the good African bone-in sort. Disappointed, I grimaced myself a plate of the remarkably red rice, red as my frustration. It blew me away. It not only shouted all the deep, sweet, meat-rich tones I craved, but also gave me the brown butter edge of the Scotch bonnet, the smoke of the paprikas, the subtle punch of the shrimps and the smug smirk of my meat-dodging host.

Smoke my squash

Serves: 4
Prep: 20 minutes
Cook: 50 minutes

Okay, so my squash of preference here is the round, dark green gem squash but you may prefer butternut. The more lacklustre they are in flavour the better. When the brazen smoked chorizo moves in, it becomes flavour karaoke.

4 whole gem squashes or
  2 butternut squash

2 tbsp olive oil

1 garlic clove, finely chopped

115g/4oz chorizo sausage,
  very finely diced

1 red pepper, deseeded and
  finely diced

¼ tsp sweet smoked paprika

75g/2½oz chopped sundried
  tomatoes

225g/8oz/1⅔ cups cooked
  long-grain white rice (or
  cook heaped ½ cup raw
  rice)

4 tbsp soft goats' cheese

1 tbsp chopped parsley
  leaves, plus extra to serve

Preheat the oven to 180°C/350°F/Gas 4.

If you are using gem squash, trim the base of each squash, so that it can stand flat, and slice off the top. Scoop out the seeds and discard them. If you use butternut squash, cut in half lengthways, scoop out the seeds and about 1cm/¾in of the flesh from the upper part. Oil a shallow baking dish with 1 tablespoon of the oil. Put the squash in the dish, cover with foil and put in the oven while you prepare the rice.

Heat the remaining oil in a deep-frying pan. Add the garlic and as it begins to soften, add the chopped chorizo. Fry over a medium heat until the red oils leach out of the sausage. Now stir in the diced pepper, smoked paprika and sundried tomatoes, then remove from the heat.

Mix the rice and cheese together in a bowl along with the chopped parsley. Now add the chorizo mixture with the oils from the frying pan and mix together well.

Remove the squash from the oven and divide the rice mixture amongst the squash. Cover again with foil and bake for about 30 minutes until the squash is tender. The squash will need about 50 minutes cooking altogether. Sprinkle with the chopped parsley and serve hot.

𝒞alcutta comforter

Truth is, we eat this with ready salted crisps and jarred pickle – a truly shameless comforter. If you have had the sophistication to buy and add the fenugreek and asafoetida, why, you deserve a happy hands-free ending.

1 tbsp vegetable or mustard oil, if you can get hold of some

1 small cauliflower, chopped into florets

90g/3¼oz/½ cup yellow split peas

2 tbsp ghee/clarified butter

1 tsp cumin seeds

1 tsp mustard seeds

1 tsp fenugreek seeds

¼ tsp asafoetida

2 bay leaves

1 tbsp grated fresh root ginger

1 large green chilli, deseeded and finely chopped

2 tomatoes, finely chopped

1 tsp turmeric

1 tbsp ground cumin

1 tbsp ground coriander

1 tsp red chilli powder

200g/7oz/heaped 1 cup long-grain white rice, rinsed and drained

salt

a handful of chopped coriander/cilantro leaves

jars of Asian pickles and crushed ready-salted crisps,

Heat ½ tablespoon of the oil in a heavy-based frying pan and sauté the cauliflower florets over a medium-high heat until they colour and soften slightly. This should take around 6–8 minutes. Remove from the pan and leave to one side.

Dry-roast the split peas over a medium heat in a separate pan for about 3–4 minutes until golden brown, then remove from heat and leave to one side.

Heat the remaining oil and the ghee together in a large heavy-based saucepan over a medium-high heat. Add the cumin seeds, and once they crackle and begin to fizz, add the mustard seeds. Wait for the mustard seeds to turn grey and spit. Now add the fenugreek seeds and asafoetida and fry them for around 10 seconds. Throw in the bay leaves, ginger and green chilli. Sauté over a low heat for about 30 seconds.

Now add the tomatoes, turmeric, ground cumin, ground coriander and chilli powder. Pour about 60ml/2fl oz/¼ cup water into the pan and continue to cook for another minute.

Stir in the fried cauliflower florets, split peas and rice. Add 700ml/24fl oz/ 3 cups water and season with salt. Allow the dish to simmer over a low heat for 10–15 minutes. As the dish becomes almost entirely dry, remove the pan from the heat and cover with a tight-fitting lid. Leave the pan for 10 minutes and the dish is ready.

Sprinkle with chopped coriander/cilantro leaves. Serve with any Asian jarred pickles and crushed ready salted crisps! We do!

Peanut & potato flattened rice

Serves: 4
Prep: 10 minutes
Cook: 20 minutes

Flattened rice is a popular Indian ingredient known as *pauwa* or *poha*. The Indians love a long-life ingredient. These flat dry grains just need to be rehydrated and they are ready to go – rice in another guise. This dish is also the go-to breakfast of Maharashtra, served with a good sweet Indian tea.

250g/9oz/2¼ cups rice flakes (*pauwa* in Asian stores)

5 tbsp rapeseed/canola or sunflower oil

1 tsp cumin seeds

½ tsp brown mustard seeds

15 fresh curry leaves

1 large waxy potato, cut into 1cm/½in chunks

½ tsp turmeric

1 tsp salt

4 tsp white sesame seeds

100g/3½oz/¾ cup roasted unsalted peanuts, skin on

2 tsp sugar

50g/1¾oz/2 cups finely chopped coriander/cilantro leaves

2 tbsp lemon juice

THE MASALA PASTE

2 green chillies, deseeded

2 garlic cloves

5cm/2in piece of fresh root ginger, peeled and diced

a pinch of salt

First, create the masala spice paste by blitzing the ingredients in a blender or pounding with a mortar and pestle. You want a smooth paste.

Soak the rice flakes in enough warm water to cover them for 1 minute, then drain immediately.

In a large frying pan or wok, heat the oil over a medium heat. Drop in the cumin seeds and wait for them to sizzle and turn brown. Add the mustard seeds and wait for them to pop and turn grey. Now turn the heat to medium-low and add the curry leaves. They will begin to sizzle but be careful not to let them turn brown. Turn the heat to low.

Now add the potato, turmeric and salt and increase the heat to medium and cook for 5 minutes, partially covered, stirring occasionally until the potatoes start to soften.

Stir in the masala paste, sesame seeds, peanuts, sugar and half of the chopped coriander/cilantro. Now you need to turn the heat to low, cover and cook for a further 5 minutes until the potatoes have cooked through. Stir occasionally to prevent any sticking.

Now add the drained rice flakes and 2 tablespoons warm water. Stir very carefully to avoid breaking the grains too much but make sure the ingredients have combined well. Cover and cook for 2 minutes, once again stirring occasionally to prevent anything sticking to the pan.

Stir in the lemon juice and continue to cook, covered, over a low heat until the rice flakes have absorbed all the liquid. The final dish should have a dry, loose finish.

Serve hot, sprinkled with the remaining coriander/cilantro.

Serves: 4
Prep: 20 minutes
Cook: 50 minutes

A top two-handed tart

I'm a kitchen control freak and coupled with that I'm a lazy cook, not one for technical complexity. This dish combines all my phobias. Overturning a hot tart using both hands is alarming. Not knowing how the self-willed vegetables might have arranged themselves for the topping fills me with terror.
But it always works and always tastes sublime.

2 tbsp sunflower oil

1 aubergine/eggplant, sliced lengthways

1 red pepper, deseeded and cut into strips

2 tomatoes, sliced

2 tbsp olive oil

2 red onions, chopped

6 mushrooms, sliced

2 garlic cloves, chopped

200g/7oz can chopped tomatoes

1 tsp soft brown sugar

150ml/5fl oz/scant ⅔ cup white wine

1 tbsp chopped parsley leaves

225g/8oz/1⅔ cups cooked long-grain white or brown rice (or cook heaped ½ cup raw rice)

350g/12oz puff pastry

salt and freshly ground black pepper

Preheat the oven to 190°C/375°F/Gas 5 and grease a 30cm/12in shallow ovenproof dish.

Oil a frying pan with 1 tablespoon of the sunflower oil and flash-fry the aubergine/eggplant slices – we want them brown on both sides. Drain on paper towels and arrange over the bottom of the oven dish.

Add the remaining oil to the pan and fry the pepper strips over a medium heat until they brown and soften. Arrange these amongst the aubergine/eggplant slices in the oven dish, then add the sliced tomatoes amongst the aubergine/eggplant and peppers. As you upturn the tart to serve it, remember that the bottom layer will form the decoration on the top of your tart, so attempt some flair.

Now heat the olive oil in the frying pan and fry the onions, mushrooms and garlic. After 5 minutes, add the canned tomatoes and brown sugar and fry for a further 3 minutes, then add the wine and the parsley and season with salt and pepper. Bring to the boil, then stir in the cooked rice. Spoon this mixture over the arranged vegetables in the oven dish.

Roll out the puff pastry into a circle slightly larger than the oven dish. Place on top and carefully tuck the sides down into the dish so that when you turn it out, it forms an edge around the whole tart.

Bake for 30 minutes until the pastry has browned. Remove from the oven and allow the dish to cool for 5 minutes. Put a large serving plate over the oven dish and turn the whole affair over, then sigh with relief and serve.

Apple-pimped parmigiana

This is a firm family favourite of mine. It is actually quite simple to construct and the final cook yields such a satisfying bubbling centrepiece. The soft freshness of the cheeses moderate the tart sweetness of the apple tomato sauce.

4 tbsp olive oil

2 aubergines/eggplants, cut lengthways into 5 slices

1 red onion, finely chopped

1 garlic clove, chopped

400g/14oz can chopped tomatoes

2 tsp soft brown sugar

1 tsp dried thyme

120ml/4fl oz/½ cup white wine

2 green apples, peeled, cored and grated

1 tbsp chopped mint leaves, plus a sprig to serve (optional)

225g/8oz/1⅔ cups cooked long-grain white or brown rice (or cook heaped ½ cup raw rice)

115g/4oz/scant ½ cup soft goats' cheese

1 egg beaten

120ml/4fl oz/½ cup milk

100g/3½oz ricotta cheese

salt and freshly ground black pepper

Preheat the oven to 190°C/375°F/Gas 5.

Heat half the oil in a shallow pan and fry the aubergine/eggplant slices in batches until they just begin to soften. They will brown in the oven later. Drain the slices on paper towels.

Heat the remaining oil in a saucepan and fry the onion and garlic until they are softened. Add the tomatoes, brown sugar, dried thyme and white wine and allow to simmer for 5 minutes over a medium heat.

Add the grated apples and mint and cook for a further 3 minutes. Stir in the cooked rice and season with salt and pepper to taste. Transfer this rice base into a shallow baking dish.

Hold back a little of the goats' cheese to garnish at the end, then beat the remaining goats' cheese with the egg, milk and ricotta cheese to produce a thick sauce. Don't worry too much if they don't blend in perfectly. Lumps will melt during the cooking process to give pockets of intensity. Now pour this cheese sauce over the tomato base.

Arrange the aubergine/eggplant slices over the top and bake in the oven for 15–20 minutes until the dish is bubbling and the aubergines/eggplants turn golden. Spoon a dollop of the reserved goats' cheeseon top with a sprig of mint, if you like, and serve.

Risotto rice

Who would have thought Italy to be such a prolific producer of rice? Arborio from the Po Valley and the risotto Rolls Royces – Carnaroli and Maratelli – from Vercelli. These risotto grains have a very particular brief. They must be absorbent enough to take flavour but generous enough to release starch to make a creamy sauce. Remember amylose, the chemical lacking in sticky rice? Well, risotto rice needs this same deficiency – it must not hold its form too tightly.

The grain is short or medium. Classifications of superfino, semifino and fino refer not to quality but to the length and width of grain. Carnaroli is least likely to overcook but what it gains in backbone it loses in speed of cooking and absorbency. This is the delicate balance that every risotto cook seeks in a rice.

Frankly, from the point of view of a home cook, who cares? I love the laissez-faire nature of risotto creation – these purposefully unstructured, fluid dishes. Coming from the Asian culture of harsh rice judgement, it is liberation indeed to dabble in wonderful, daring flavours that can hide a multitude of textural sins. But then I don't have an Italian mother-in-law.

Unlike a paella, risotto requires stirring. The risotto grains require agitation by the chef to draw out the rice's creamy starches.

How to cook risotto rice

* Use 1 cup of rice to just under 2 cups of liquid (190g/6¾oz rice to 450ml/15fl oz water).

* Put the rice in a colander and rinse under cold running water until the water runs clear. Leave to drain.

* Put the rice in a saucepan and heat gently, then gradually being to add hot cooking liquid (stock, wine or water), stirring it into the pan a ladleful at a time and waiting for it to be absorbed before adding more. It takes about 20 minutes before the rice is tender and creamy but still with a bit of bite.

* Leave to stand for 5 minutes before serving.

Gold leaf & white truffle risotto

Serves: 4
Prep: 10 minutes
Cook: 30 minutes

Behold, the lily gilded! This is rice at its most hedonsitic. Jaws drop, faces flush as this dish dives straight into the endorphins. Not a rainy Tuesday supper, unless you are Marie Antoinette. Don't be put off by the gold leaf – you can buy it in delicatessens or online for the same price as a bag of rice. To get the most out of the truffle, bury it in your rice jar the day before you cook for the ultimate truffle kick. If you can't stretch to a truffle, give the risotto a good drizzle of truffle oil when you finish.

60g/2¼oz/4 tbsp cold butter, cubed

1 white onion, very finely diced

350g/12oz/scant 2 cups superfine risotto rice, preferably Carnaroli, rinsed and drained

120ml/4fl oz/½ cup dry white wine

1.5 litres/52fl oz/6½ cups good-quality hot chicken stock

30g/1oz/scant ½ cup freshly grated Parmesan cheese

1½ tbsp white truffle oil

½ brown truffle

4cm/1½in square of edible gold leaf, torn into tiny pieces

salt and freshly ground black pepper

Dig out a heavy-based saucepan – risotto needs this for an even heat distribution. Add the butter and melt over a very low heat. Add the onion and cook for 5 minutes as we want them soft and translucent and certainly not browned at all.

Increase the heat to medium and add the rice, tossing the grains in the butter and onions.

Now add the wine and stir on a medium heat until almost all the wine has disappeared. Now add the chicken stock one ladleful at a time, stirring until each one is absorbed before adding more. This should take about 20 minutes. The risotto is done when the grains or rice are tender but with a slightly nutty core.

Remove the risotto from the heat and allow it to sit for a minute unstirred. Now, quickly beat in the Parmesan with some vigour. Once combined to an oozing satisfaction, stir in the truffle oil. Check the seasoning, adding a little more salt and pepper to taste

Serve the risotto in four shallow dishes as quickly as possible. Shave a little brown truffle over each one and sprinkle with tiny pieces of gold leaf before serving.

Serves: 4
Prep: 30 minutes
Cook: 1 hour
10 minutes

Emerald rice bake

Pastry, rice, spinach – thudding earthy ingredients. Feta, squash and onion bring this pie lift and light. The colours are beautiful, the flavours tick every box.

320g/11¼oz shortcrust pastry

a little flour, for dusting

3 tbsp olive oil

½ butternut squash (top half), skin on, very thinly sliced

1 large onion, chopped

1 garlic clove, chopped

175g/6oz washed chopped fresh/tinned/frozen spinach

4 eggs

75g/2½oz feta cheese, diced

40g/1½oz/scant ½ cup freshly grated Parmesan cheese

4 tbsp Greek yogurt, plus extra to serve

6 tbsp whole milk

225g/8oz/1⅔ cups leftover cooked rice (any grain/ any colour! Or cook scant ½ cup raw rice)

salt and freshly ground black pepper

Preheat the oven to 180°C/350°F/Gas 4.

Roll out the pastry thinly on a lightly floured work surface and use to line a 25cm/10in flan ring. Prick the base with a fork and bake in the oven for 12 minutes.

Heat a frying pan over a medium-high heat, add half the oil and fry the thinly sliced butternut squash on both sides until soft. Leave to one side.

Add the remaining oil to the pan and fry the onion and garlic on a medium-low heat for 5 minutes. You want them translucent, not brown.

Combine the spinach, eggs, cheeses, yogurt, milk and onion and garlic mixture. Season well with salt and pepper. Now add the cooked rice and mix carefully but thoroughly.

Transfer this rice mixture to the flan base and bake for 15 minutes. Remove from the oven and arrange the fried squash circles on the top. Bake for a further 20 minutes or until the whole pie is lightly browned.

Serve hot or cold with a Greek yogurt dip.

Black beet burgers

Sweet and full of earthy umami, I sampled these burgers in a London gastro pub and never forgot them. I played with many permutations of the ingredients and this is the version that worked best.

Serves: 4

Prep: 45 minutes, plus chilling

Cook: 1 hour 10 minutes

1 large red beetroot/beet

100g/3½oz/scant ½ cup long-grain brown rice, soaked for 2 hours, rinsed and drained

2 tbsp olive oil, plus extra for frying

1 small onion, finely chopped

2 garlic cloves, crushed

1 tbsp cider vinegar

400g/14oz canned black beans, drained and rinsed

25g/1oz/scant ¼ cup pitted prunes, chopped

1 tsp wholegrain mustard

½ tbsp sweet smoked paprika

½ tsp ground cumin

¼ tsp ground coriander

½ tsp thyme leaves

150g/5½oz/1½ cups rolled oats, blitzed to a fine powder

1 egg yolk

2 slices of cheese (optional)

salt and freshly ground black pepper

soft burger buns

Preheat the oven to 200°C/400°F/Gas 6. Wrap the beetroot/beet loosely in foil and roast for 50–60 minutes until soft. Leave to one side.

Meanwhile, bring the rice, 240ml/8fl oz/1 cup water and 1 teaspoon salt to the boil, then reduce the heat and simmer for 25–30 minutes until the water has been absorbed. Cover tightly, remove from the heat and set aside to cool.

Heat half the olive oil in a frying pan over a medium-high heat. Add the onion and a pinch of salt and cook until golden brown. Add the garlic and continue to fry over a medium-low heat until the onions are a crisp brown. Add the vinegar and stir it in with any dark residue in the pan. Simmer, stirring, until the vinegar is reduced entirely, then remove from the heat.

Add half the beans to the food processor with the prunes and pulse until they are roughly chopped, NOT a fine paste. Put in a bowl and add the remaining whole beans.

Remove the skin from the cooled roasted beet using the side of a spoon. Grate the beetroot/beet into a sieve/strainer set over a bowl, then gently press the gratings to remove as much of the liquid as possible.

Add the beetroot/beet, cooked rice and sautéed onions to the bowl with the beans. Add the rest of the olive oil, the mustard, smoked paprika, cumin, coriander and thyme. Mix well and season with salt and pepper to taste. Finally, mix in the ground oats and egg. Cover with cling film/plastic wrap, and refrigerate for at least 2 hours, or overnight.

Scoop up a handful of the mixture and shape it between your palms into a thick patty the size of your buns. You can make 4 large or 8 small patties.

Heat a cast-iron or heavy-based frying pan over a high heat. Add a few tablespoons of oil to coat the bottom of the pan. When hot, add the burgers and cook for 2 minutes until they develop a good crust, then turn them over to cook the other side. Push back any pieces that break off – these burgers are about flavour not tidiness. Cook for another 2 minutes, then cover the pan and reduce the heat to medium-low. Cook for 4 more minutes until the patties are heated through.

If you want, lay slices of cheese over the burgers for the last minute of cooking. Serve on burger buns.

4

Souped-up sides

Super support acts

Serves: 4
Prep: 5 minutes
Cook: 40 minutes

Lemon & olive rice

Mediterranean flavours – the stuff of trestle tables under an olive-grove canopy. You could imagine it with a fresh, fragrant casserole on the table as a tempting starter for your meal. Then simply shave a good, white, crisp sheep's cheese onto it, sit back and feel the sun on your neck.

1 tbsp olive oil

1 onion, finely chopped

2 garlic cloves, crushed

300g/10½oz/heaped
1½ cups short-grain
brown rice, soaked for
2 hours, rinsed and drained

2 thyme sprigs

1 bay leaf

100g/3½oz/scant ½ cup
pitted green olives, sliced

2 tbsp chopped basil leaves

1½ tbsp fresh lemon juice

½ tbsp lemon zest

1 tbsp extra virgin olive oil,
for drizzling

salt and freshly ground black
pepper

Heat the olive oil in a large saucepan. Add the onion and garlic and cook over a medium heat for about 8 minutes, stirring occasionally, until softened.

Add the rice, thyme, bay leaf and 450ml/16fl oz/2 cups water and bring to the boil. Boil for 1 minute, then remove from the heat, cover and leave to stand for 30 minutes.

Add ½ teaspoon salt to the rice. Cover and simmer over a low heat, stirring occasionally, until most of the water has been absorbed, about 30 minutes. Remove from the heat and discard the bay leaf and thyme.

Stir in the olives, chopped basil and lemon juice and zest and season with salt and pepper.

Spoon the rice into bowls and drizzle with extra virgin olive oil to serve.

Coconut & sweet onion rice

This is one of my very favourite rice dishes. A sweet coconut affair, the browning of the onion is critical – ribbons of caramel chew just add to the sweet-shop thrill of this splendid side dish.

2 tbsp sunflower oil

2 small onions, cut into fine rings

350g/12oz/1¾ cups Thai fragrant rice, rinsed and drained

400ml/14fl oz/scant 2 cups coconut milk

1 tsp sugar

1 lemongrass stalk, bruised

5cm/2in cinnamon stick

salt

Heat the oil in a heavy-based frying pan over a medium heat and fry the onions until they are brown and crispy. Leave to one side.

Put the rice in a large saucepan with the coconut milk, sugar, lemongrass, cinnamon and 300ml/10½fl oz/1¼ cups water. Season with salt, bring to the boil, then boil briskly for about 5 minutes.

Now turn the heat down and simmer the rice for a further 10 minutes. Once the liquid is absorbed and the rice looks almost dry, put a tight lid on the pan and turn off the heat. Leave the pan to stand for a further 10 minutes.

Toss the sweet, crisp onions through the rice, discard the cinnamon and lemongrass and serve.

Jamaican rice & peas

The Jamaican Sunday favourite – it is the thyme and coconut that define this excellent side dish. The 'peas' are kidney beans and canned are fine. Scotch bonnet is good too, if you can bear it. They give a wonderful, butter-peppered heat. I had my first Scotch bonnet served this way at a Jamaican pal's home, and I will never forget that first hit. Many tries it took, to get close to recreating that first rice and peas buzz. This recipe, for me, nails that pesky dragon.

Serves: 4
Prep: 10 minutes
Cook: 25 minutes

3½ tbsp sunflower oil

2 spring onions/scallions
   or 1 small onion, chopped

1 garlic clove, crushed

300g/10½oz/1¼ cups
   long-grain white rice,
   rinsed and drained

400ml/14fl oz/1⅔ cups
   coconut milk

1 whole Scotch bonnet
   (optional)

400g/14oz can kidney beans,
   rinsed and drained

3 tbsp chopped thyme
   leaves

salt and freshly ground black
   pepper

Heat the oil in a frying pan and fry the spring onions/scallions and garlic until translucent.

Add the rice and stir well, then add the coconut milk and 400ml/14fl oz/1⅔ cups water. Then add your whole, unpunctured Scotch bonnet, if you like, and bring to the boil.

Now add the kidney beans and thyme, cover and simmer for about 20 minutes until the rice is cooked. Season with the salt and freshly ground black pepper to taste.

A Sunday is not a Sunday

Rice and peas is a mainstay of Jamaican cuisine. A Sunday is not a Sunday without rice and peas, is how the saying goes.

The truth is that like every good food-loving culture, the Jamaicans are judgemental. If you don't serve rice and peas on a Sunday it means that you were too lazy to start the marathon prep that soaks up one's Saturday night, washing and soaking the kidney beans and infusing them with garlic.

The tradition and the dish have taken on a profound and almost sanctified position in the Jamaican kitchen and, indeed, the Jamaican psyche. I remember well the outrage and public revolt at an advert for stock cubes that featured a very famous, foul-mouthed TV chef ... yes, I know that does not narrow things down much! However, he rather hilariously created his Jamaican-inspired rice and peas using ... wait for it ... brown rice and ... garden peas. This achieved both insult and injury in a one-pot dish. Public meltdown ensued and a prompt removal of the advert was the result. This was sacrilege, they screamed. And that is how seriously the Jamaicans take their rice and peas.

Ginger, clove & black cardamom rice

Black cardamom is worth investing in if you want to make really good fried rice. Weird, gnarled, almost medicinal black shrivels, they do something remarkable to rice when they are cooked together in this delicious side dish. Clove and cardamom are woody and aromatic big hitters and they form a gorgeous frame for the earthy subtlety of the musky brown basmati.

1 tbsp groundnut oil

3 black cardamom pods

6 whole cloves

225g/8oz/1¼ cups brown basmati rice, soaked for 2 hours, rinsed and drained

350ml/12fl oz/1½ cups vegetable stock

2.5cm/1in piece of fresh root ginger, finely sliced

5cm/2in piece of pared lemon zest

Heat the oil in a saucepan to a medium-high heat. Drop in the black cardamom pods and cloves and allow them to sizzle for 1 minute.

Now add the washed rice grains and toss them in the oil with the whole spices for 1 minute.

Now pour in the stock. Add the ginger and lemon zest and bring the pan slowly to the boil. Turn the heat down, cover and cook very gently for 20–25 minutes until the rice is tender and all the water has been absorbed.

Cover with a tightly fitting lid and turn off the heat. Leave the pan undisturbed for 10 minutes, then serve hot.

Spiced coriander rice

Serves: 4
Prep: 10 minutes
Cook: 20 minutes

There is some heat and some spice to this dish. Ironically, it works best when served with mild or subtle main dishes. To reduce the heat, reduce the amount of chilli you use in the opening stages.

2 green chillies, deseeded

1–2 garlic cloves

2 handfuls of chopped coriander/cilantro leaves

3½ tbsp sunflower oil

½ tsp cumin seeds

½ tsp mustard seeds

250g/9oz/scant 1½ cups white basmati rice, rinsed and drained

salt

In a food processor, blend together the chillies, garlic and coriander/cilantro with a pinch of salt. Add a touch of water if you need to loosen the mixture to allow the processor to produce a fine paste.

Heat the oil in a saucepan over a medium-high heat. Once it starts to shimmer, add the cumin and mustard seeds. As soon as they finish popping but before the cumin seeds turn dark brown, remove the pan from the heat. Now quickly toss in the rice and stir off the heat for 1 minute.

Return the pan to a medium heat and add the green spice paste and ½ teaspoon salt. Pour over 1 litre/35fl oz/4⅓cups water and stir gently. Bring the pan to the boil and simmer for 10 minutes until all the water has been absorbed.

Now clamp a tight lid onto the pan and remove it from the heat. Leave the rice for at least 10 minutes with the lid undisturbed, before forking it loose and serving.

Lemongrass & lime Thai rice

Serves: 4
Prep: 10 minutes
Cook: 45 minutes

I like to use brown rice in this light, fragrant dish – the shrill lemongrass and lime sit well on the wholesome depth of the heavier grain, which makes a lovely contrast with all kinds of main courses.

1 tbsp sunflower oil

1 onion, finely chopped

1 lemongrass stalk, just the lower tender portion, finely chopped

grated zest of 2 limes

1½ tsp coriander seeds

250g/9oz/1⅓ cups long-grain brown rice, soaked for 2 hours, rinsed and drained

625ml/21½fl oz/2⅔ cups vegetable stock

4 tbsp chopped coriander/cilantro leaves

1 lime, cut into wedges

Heat the oil in a saucepan and add the onion, lemongrass, lime zest and coriander seeds and fry gently over a low heat for 3 minutes.

Now add the drained rice and toss in the oil for 2 minutes. Pour the stock over the top and bring the pan to the boil, stirring occasionally.

Turn the heat to very low and cover the pan. Cook for 30 minutes until the rice is soft and the liquid absorbed fully. Turn off the heat and leave, tightly covered, for 10 minutes.

Before serving, fork the chopped coriander/cilantro through the rice and serve with lime wedges.

Pine nut pimped pilau

Pilau is just what Indians do to their rice when they have visitors. There is no formula – each home will have their own combination of spices and their own take on the recipe. The addition of pine nuts is something I devised as I loved the way the pine nuts mimicked the rice grains but offered an entirely different bite. It messed with my head a little.

1 heaped tbsp pine nuts

2 tbsp sunflower oil

½ tsp cumin seeds

4 cloves

2 black cardamom pods

1 bay leaf

1 cinnamon stick

1 onion, finely sliced

300g/10½oz/1½ cups white basmati rice

½ tsp turmeric

½ tsp salt

Heat a dry frying pan to a medium heat and toss the pine nuts until they become browned and evenly toasted. Remove from the pan and leave to one side.

Heat the oil in a saucepan over a medium-high heat. Add the cumin seeds and as soon as they fizz and turn brown, add the cloves, cardamom, bay leaf and cinnamon and stir for 30 seconds. Add the sliced onion and turn the heat down to medium. Add the onion and fry until golden brown.

Now add the rice, unwashed, and toss in the aromatic spiced oil. After 1 minute, add 680ml/23½fl oz/scant 3 cups water, the turmeric and salt. Bring to the boil, then turn the heat to medium-low and simmer for about 15–20 minutes until the water is almost all absorbed.

Now clamp a tight lid on the pan and switch off the heat. Leave the pan to stand for 10 minutes, then sprinkle with the toasted pine nuts to serve.

Carrot cardamom pots

Very much a savoury dish, although your eyes lead you down thoughts of rice pudding and carrot halwa. This is a piece of Persian ingenuity – a brave, savoury milk rice that hijacks all the benefits of Eastern fragranced exoticism with the good homely crust of your nan's rice pud. These little pots work particularly well with grilled/broiled and barbecue-style meats, or dishes with a dry Eastern slant.

1 tbsp butter, plus extra for greasing

180g/6¼oz/1 cup short-grain rice, soaked for 2 hours, rinsed and drained

320g/11¼oz carrots, peeled and grated

1 tsp cardamom pods, crushed

1 tsp ground coriander

¼ tsp freshly grated nutmeg

1 tsp salt

300ml/10½fl oz/1¼ cups whole milk

Preheat the oven to 180°C/350°F/Gas 4 and grease four individual ovenproof dishes or a large baking dish.

Put the rice in a large mixing bowl. Mix in all the other ingredients except the milk and butter.

Spoon the rice mixture into the prepared baking dishes and shake them to ensure an even spread. Now carefully pour in the milk and dot the tops with little pieces of butter. Put the dishes in the oven and cook for 30 minutes for smaller pots or 45 for a larger one. You want a golden brown crust on the top and, hopefully, one on the bottom as well.

Remove from oven and allow to cool a little before serving. The dish can be served warm or cold.

Serves: 4
Prep: 10 minutes
Cook: 40 minutes

Rice & onion dauphinoise

Creamy and uncompromising, the best one can do to salve one's conscience is use brown rice – it adds a better bite to something that is otherwise almost too unctuously, oozingly easy to down.

1 tbsp olive oil, plus extra for greasing

4 small onions, chopped

200g/7oz/1¼ cups cooked long-grain brown rice (or cook ½ cup raw rice)

120ml/2fl oz/½ cup whole milk

150g/5½oz Swiss cheese, grated

¼ tsp salt

¼ tsp ground black pepper

a pinch of allspice

40g/1½oz/½ cup freshly grated Parmesan cheese

2 tbsp chopped parsley leaves

Preheat the oven to 170°C/325°F/gas 3 and spray a 20cm/8in square glass or ceramic baking dish with cooking spray.

Heat a large frying pan over a medium-high heat, add the oil and swirl to coat the base of the pan. Add the onions and fry for 5 minutes or until soft. Transfer to a large bowl.

Stir the rice, milk, Swiss cheese, salt, pepper and allspice into the onions, then spoon the mixture into the prepared dish. Sprinkle with Parmesan cheese, cover with foil and bake for 30 minutes.

Uncover and bake for an additional 5 minutes, or until the cheese begins to brown. Top with parsley to serve.

Parmesan, sage & Riesling risotto

Serves: 4
Prep: 10 minutes
Cook: 25 minutes

There is, in my view, nothing wrong with planning this rewarding, luxurious dish around an open bottle of leftover Riesling. Indeed a tired bottle of dry white wine could not limp towards a finer ending. Use the best Parmesan that you can get hold of and grate it just before you mix it into the rice. This works brilliantly served as an accompaniment to fish and seafood dishes.

55g/2oz/4 tbsp cold butter, cubed

1 white onion, very finely diced

400g/14oz/scant 2¼ cups superfine risotto rice, preferably Carnaroli rice, rinsed and drained

125ml/4fl oz/½ cup Riesling or dry white wine

2.5 litres/88fl oz/10 cups good-quality hot chicken stock

2 tsp chopped sage leaves, plus extra to serve

1 tsp salt

30g/1oz/scant ½ cup freshly grated Parmesan cheese

freshly ground black pepper

Dig out a heavy based pan – risotto needs this for an even heat distribution. Add the butter and melt over a medium heat.

Add the onion and cook over a very low heat for 5 minutes – we want it soft and translucent and certainly not browned at all. Increase the heat to medium and add the rice, tossing the grains in the butter and onion.

Now add the wine and stir on a high heat until almost all the wine has disappeared. Turn the heat to medium and begin to add the stock one ladleful at a time, stirring until each one is absorbed before adding any more. This should take about 20 minutes. The risotto is done when the grains of rice are tender but with a slightly nutty core. Add the sage and season with salt and pepper just as the rice is cooked.

Remove the risotto from the heat and allow it to sit for a minute unstirred. Now, quickly beat in the Parmesan with some vigour. Check the seasoning, adding a little more salt and pepper to taste.

Serve the risotto as quickly as possible as it will continue to cook even as it rests. Finish with a slither of velvet green sage to serve.

Serves: 4–6
Prep: 10 minutes
Cook: 50 minutes

Serious carb-on-carb action

This wonderful meat-free, nay, vegan Indian side dish is full of flavour, bringing an excited, spiced chatter from the side of the plate. It is perfect served with grilled/broiled, plain, brutally succulent meats.

200g/7oz/1¼ cups white basmati rice, rinsed and drained

3 tbsp sunflower oil

1 tsp mustard seeds

1 green finger chilli, deseeded and chopped

1 onion, chopped

3 potatoes, peeled and cut into 5mm/¼in pieces

70g/2½oz curly kale or any strong dark greens, sliced

1 tsp turmeric

1 tsp salt

juice ½ small lemon

1 tsp clear honey

2 tbsp chopped coriander/ cilantro leaves

Put the rice in a saucepan, add 480ml/16fl oz/2 cups water and bring to the boil. Reduce to a medium heat and simmer for 10–15 minutes until all the water has been absorbed.

Remove from the heat and put a tightly fitting lid on the pan. Leave for 10 minutes.

Meanwhile, heat the oil in a large saucepan and once it begins to smoke, add the mustard seeds. They will pop dramatically. Add the chilli and onion. Turn down the heat to medium and fry the onion until just translucent.

Now add the potatoes, kale, turmeric, salt and 120ml/4fl oz/½ cup water. Mix well, bring to the boil, then cover and cook over a low heat for 15 minutes until the potatoes are soft.

Mix the cooked rice into the potatoes and stir carefully. Add the lemon juice and a little more salt to taste, if needed, and mix well. Cook for a further 2 minutes, then add the honey, drizzling it all over the potatoes and stirring it in carefully.

Turn onto a serving plate and sprinkle with the coriander/cilantro to serve.

No need to be a purist

The Indians are remarkably purist in their rice cooking. They are not quick to embrace the various colours, forms and consistencies of rice in the way we in the West have.

They are big fans of good, white basmati rice that should be as white as snow and smell a little of musk. The wild rices, black, red and brown rices of the world are looked at askance. The highly elastic, starch-addled sticky rices loved by so many across Asia – are seen as a downright comedy carb in the eyes of many Indians. Strange isn't it? It might be a case of if it ain't broke, then why fix it. The white, elegant musk of eyes down, obedient basmati works as a meek and humble foil for the powerful, brassy might of Indian curries. Indians really don't want the flavour of rice to interfere with the delicate balance of spices. Brown rice and red rice have far too much to say.

What has also dawned on me over the years, as I stray into other rice cultures, is the reluctance of Indians to cook rice with other ingredients, to adulterate it, so to speak. Stand-alone fried rice will be lightly adorned with cardamom, cumin, saffron, perhaps nuts and raisins to finish. Biryani is where rice is wrestled into the shadows of meats and spices and onions and all that is dominant. But this method of one-pot cooking is a rare observance in the Indian kitchen.

It is because I am less of a rice purist – essentially lazy and more of a lover of the single centerpiece meal – that I often put together dishes like this Serious Carb-on-Carb Action. Here I use kale, because it is beautiful and robust, but I usually make this dish with whatever lies limp and sorry in my veg rack. Rice, in all her elegant glory, brings the flaccid back to life.

Wild rice

Wild rice is a cousin of and not related directly to Asian rice. It comes, instead, from a species of grass. I always feel a bit wanton using this type of rice in any great quantity. I use it in dishes like my Killer Cucumber & Wild Rice Salad (see opposite) and paired with red rice in my Black & Red Rice Boudoir Salad (see page 176) where it goes a long way in terms of texture and contrast. It should not always be relegated to the cold ranks of salad, and I always feel it seems a touch needy mixing it with white rice, like a token edible status symbol. These economic and philosophical shackles aside, it tastes seriously good. It gives salads bite and flavour. It adds a good crunch and an aesthetic charm to white rice.

Also known as Canadian or Indian rice, this grain was loved by the Native Americans. Long and thin with black husks, it is an expensive delicacy as it has been grown in small quantities, hailing from wild shallow waters, with only the flower head protruding. The Chinese are only interested in eating the stem of the plant. I dare say they struggle with the same anti-bourgeois hang-ups as I do.

How to cook wild rice

* Use 1 cup of rice to just under 4 cups of water (190g/6¾oz rice to 900ml/31fl oz water).

* Put the rice and water in a saucepan. Bring to the boil, then simmer gently for about 50 minutes, uncovered, until just tender and almost dry.

* Cover tightly, remove from the heat and leave to stand for 20 minutes.

How to cook wild & brown or white rice mix

* Wild rice works very well mixed with a brown rice, which has more of an organic 21st-century feel than the stark 1980's black and white.

* An attractive mix is 1 cup of white/brown rice to ⅓ cup wild rice. This mix will need just over 3 cups of water (2 for the white, 1 for the wild).

* Keep the colours separate and start by boiling the wild rice in 480ml/16fl oz/2 cups water. I like to give it a 15-minute head start to avoid the needle-like quality it can have against softer grains.

* Then add the white/brown grains and 250ml/9fl oz/generous 1 cup water, partially cover and simmer for 35 minutes or so until almost dry.

* Cover tightly, remove from the heat and leave to stand for 20 minutes.

Killer cucumber & wild rice salad

Serves: 4
Prep: 20 minutes, plus chilling
Cook: 40 minutes

It is best to use a mandoline to slice the cucumbers – you really do want a very soft, curled, liquor-rich cucumber mass. The salt is used to flavour, but also to draw the liquid out of the cucumbers. It is the sharp, sweet, cleansing tang of this salad's liquor that will drive you to demolish it in minutes. This is a fantastic Eastern European salad that is used as an accompaniment to heavy meat dishes. The liquor that is produced in the combination of the cucumber juices – sweet, sharp and salty – is utterly addictive.

115g/4oz/½ cup wild rice, rinsed and drained

2 cucumbers, peeled and very finely sliced

6 tbsp distilled vinegar

1 tsp salt

2 tbsp white sugar

1 tsp garlic purée

½ tsp paprika

1 tbsp chopped dill

3 tbsp sour cream

Put the wild rice in a heavy-based saucepan and cover with water. Bring to the boil, then simmer for 30–40 minutes, checking the rice frequently. Once it is cooked but al dente, drain and rinse with cold water to stop the cooking process. Leave to one side.

Take a large salad bowl and add the cucumbers and all the other ingredients except the dill and the sour cream. Mix thoroughly. Do not be afraid of the cucumber becoming soft and leaching out its water. This is the aim and texture you are looking for.

Now add the wild rice. Stir in gently and put the salad in the refrigerator for around 1 hour. Truth be told, I have always eaten this freshly tossed and unrefrigerated, but allowing it to rest in the refrigerator increases the absorption of the juices into the rice grains.

Before serving, stir in the sour cream and sprinkle the chopped dill over the salad. Serve in a small bowl and don't try to pretend that it's not all about the killer liquor.

Black & red rice boudoir salad

This centrepiece salad has all the pimped splendour of an Arabian boudoir. It has the uncompromising flavour punch of an oriental night market but a bejewelled elegant beauty that will complement many a main-course meal.

1 tbsp groundnut oil

120g/4¼oz/heaped ½ cup wild rice

250g/9oz/1⅓ cups red rice, preferably Camargue, rinsed and drained

55g/2oz/heaped ⅓ cup chopped pitted dates

80g/2¾oz/1 cup flaked/ slivered almonds

2 spring onions/scallions, finely chopped

1 red onion, finely diced

25g/1oz/¼ cup pecans, roughly chopped

55g/2oz/heaped ⅓ cup pistachios, chopped

1 sharp red eating apple, cored and finely diced

1 small yellow pepper, deseeded and finely diced

seeds of ½ pomegranate

CORIANDER DRESSING

2 small garlic cloves, peeled

1 small green chilli, deseeded

40g/1½oz/¾ cup coriander/ cilantro leaves, chopped, plus extra leaves to serve

½ tsp salt

3 tbsp lemon juice

2 tbsp freshly squeezed orange juice

2 tbsp clear honey

4 tbsp olive oil

To make the dressing, blitz the garlic, chilli, coriander/cilantro, salt, lemon juice, orange juice and honey in a blender. With the motor running, gradually drizzle in the olive oil. Leave to one side.

Heat half the oil in a pan and, when it is hot, toss in the wild rice grains and stir to coat in the oil. Add 230ml/7¾fl oz/scant 1 cup boiling water and cook over a gentle heat, covered, for 50 minutes.

Meanwhile, heat the remaining oil in a pan and toss in the red rice grains. Add 570ml/20fl oz/2½ cups boiling water and cook over a gentle heat, covered, for 20 minutes.

Lift the lid and stir the chopped dates in with the red rice. Replace the lid and continue to cook gently for a further 20 minutes, then switch off the heat and let the rice stand for a further 10 minutes.

In a hot dry frying pan, toast the almonds until they are slightly brown.

Once both rices are cooked, toss them together and add one-third of the salad dressing.

Wait for the rice to cool to room temperature, then stir in the remainder of the salad dressing followed by the spring onions/scallions, red onion, pecans, pistachios, apple and pepper.

Sprinkle the pomegranate seeds, toasted almonds and coriander/cilantro leaves over the top just before serving.

Chilled rice raita

Serves: 4
Prep: 15 minutes
Cook: 40 minutes

Rice raita is a very common salve to the delicate Indian stomach. It is comfort food, a panacea. Yogurt is seen as the ultimate antibiotic and rice as the god of small intestines. Okay, so that's where this dish sits medicinally but it also tastes amazing – refreshing and zingy served alongside curries and breads.

200g/7oz/1¼ cups long-grain brown or basmati rice, rinsed and drained
½ tbsp flaked/slivered almonds to garnish
1 tbsp sunflower oil
½ tsp mustard seeds
½ tsp cumin seeds
a pinch of asafoetida (optional)
1 small green finger chilli, deseeded and chopped
480g/1lb 1oz/2¼ cups yogurt
1 tsp salt
½ tsp freshly ground black pepper
½ tsp ground cinnamon

Put the rice in a large saucepan and add 500ml/17fl oz/2 cups water to cover and bring to the boil. Reduce to a medium heat and simmer for 20-25 minutes until all the water has been absorbed. Remove from the heat and put a tightly fitting lid on the pan. Leave for 10 minutes.

Toast the almond flakes in a dry pan, then leave to one side once they are lightly browned.

Heat the oil in a deep saucepan. Add the mustard and cumin seeds. They will begin to pop and splutter. Now add the asafoetida and the green chilli. After a few seconds, remove from the heat.

Put the cooked rice in a large mixing bowl. Pour the spiced oil over the rice and stir carefully and thoroughly.

Add the yogurt, salt, pepper and cinnamon until combined thoroughly, then chill until ready to serve. Sprinkle the toasted almonds on top.

5

Happy endings

The rice sweet elite

Saffron almond meringue puds

Serves: 4
Prep: 5 minutes
Cook: 30 minutes

A bitter sweet symphony, that's almond and saffron. They work perfectly together as each of them skirts around both arrogantly acrid and rarefied floral notes. I love the foil of a thuddingly humble rice pudding foundation and the fairytale fluff of the meringue. This is such a quick pudding and will make you look rather clever for creating both Alhambran elegance and those darn tricksy soft peaks.

5 saffron strands

750ml/26fl oz/3¼ cups whole milk

200g/7oz/heaped 1 cup pudding rice, rinsed and drained

400ml/14fl oz/1⅔ cups double/heavy cream

150g/5½oz/¾ cup caster/granulated sugar

1 tbsp almond extract

3 egg whites

3 tbsp flaked/slivered almonds, lightly toasted

Preheat the grill/broiler to medium-high.

Put the saffron strands in a small flameproof dish and put under the grill/broiler for 2 minutes. Now remove and crumble the threads into the milk.

Put the rice and two-thirds of the cream into a heavy-based pan and cook over a medium heat for 2–3 minutes, stirring occasionally.

Now add the milk and 2 tablespoons of the sugar to the pan and continue to cook over a low heat for a further 10–15 minutes. You are waiting for the rice grains to become soft. When the liquid has almost entirely disappeared, add the remaining cream along with the almond extract.

Whisk the egg whites in a separate, grease-free bowl until they form soft peaks. Add the remaining sugar and continue to whisk until stiff to create the meringue.

Pour the almond rice pudding into flameproof ramekins and spoon or pipe the meringue mixture on top of each pudding. Grill/broil for 3–5 minutes until the tops of the meringues begin to turn golden, then sprinkle the flaked/slivered almonds over the tops and serve straight away.

Chilli, ginger & mango crumble

Mangos – creamy and sweetly obliging – take the irk of the chilli graciously in their custardy stride. The chilli gives this otherwise saccharine ride a welcome, dangerous edge. Remember, the longer the chilli, the milder it is. Hence, finger chilli is a good medium heat; The bird's eye, a hot little blighter. The secret to the perfumed, endorphin-grabbing buzz from this crumble is using Alphonso or Kesar mango pulp if you possibly can. You can get it in any Asian grocers and I urge you to introduce yourself to this, the best kept dessert secret of the Asian kitchen.

100g/3½oz/½ cup caster/
   granulated sugar
3 mangos, peeled, pitted and
   diced
½ pineapple, peeled, cored
   and diced
5cm/2in piece of fresh root
   ginger, peeled and grated
400g/14oz canned Alphonso
   or Kesar mango pulp
½ red finger chilli, deseeded
   and finely chopped
grated zest and juice of 1 lime
45g/1¾oz/3 tbsp unsalted
   butter
cream or ice cream

THE CRUMBLE
50g/1¾oz/⅓ cup rice flour
175g/6oz/1⅓ cups plain/
   all-purpose flour
100g/3½oz/scant ½ cup
   unsalted butter
a pinch of salt
75g/2½oz/heaped ⅓ cup
   soft brown sugar
½ tsp ground cinnamon
50g/1¾oz/heaped ⅓ cup
   almonds and/or cashew
   nuts, roughly chopped

Preheat the oven to 220°C/425°F/Gas 7.

To caramelize the fruit, heat the sugar in a heavy-based saucepan and once it dissolves and starts to turn a gentle brown, add the mango and pineapple pieces, the ginger, mango pulp, chilli and the lime zest and juice. Stir gently, then add the butter a small piece at a time.

Allow to cook for 2 minutes over a medium heat until the sauce thickens to a syrup-like consistency. Remove from the heat and transfer the mixture to an ovenproof baking dish.

To make the crumble, put all the ingredients except the nuts into a food processor and blend until you have a fine breadcrumb consistency. Now transfer this mixture to a bowl and stir in the chopped almonds or cashews – you can use a combination of both or simply one type of nut.

Sprinkle the nut crumble mixture on top of the fruit and bake for 20–25 minutes until golden brown and bubbling. Serve hot with cream or ice cream.

Pudding rice

A very English concept, these fat, round, shiny grains look almost tapioca-like. Is that how they fit so perfectly into our pudding shelves and psyche? They are basically short-grain white rice grains packaged as 'pudding rice'. They are not a specific type of grain. They are easy to spot – winking, glossy, almost round, pearls. Outside of England, the name 'pudding rice' does not really exist.

I think it sweet, this grand title of 'pudding rice' given to the humble short-grain in Britain. They are right to be proud of what this stumpy little darling can do in sugar and milk. I have used it in many of my dessert rice dishes unless I felt that the recipe or provenance demanded something altogether different.

For desserts, Indians swear by long, needle-like basmati rice to produce their fragrant, aromatic rice pudding dishes. Those with Italian heritage love the Arborio creaminess in their desserts. Many South East Asians will use sticky or sushi rice in their puddings. None is wrong.

The general technique below is to demonstrate how it is cooked – not made into a dessert. It is important to know how a rice is generally cooked, how it reacts to water and heat so that you understand more about the nature of the rice type. It is with this understanding that one can deploy it and interchange it with gay abandon.

How to cook pudding rice

* Use 1 cup of rice to just over 2 cups of liquid (190g/6¾oz rice to 535ml/18¾fl oz water).

* Put the rice in a saucepan and add the water. Bring to the boil, then simmer over the very lowest heat, or bake in a very low oven for about 2 hours, uncovered, until creamy.

* Cover tightly, remove from the heat and leave to stand for 20 minutes.

Juniper & lemon curd rice pudding

This is such a simple dish, you can even construct it wearing an anorak before you head out for a long drizzly walk and it will beckon you home like a herbal, lemony, come-hither light on your doorstep.

Serves: 4
Prep: 10 minutes
Cook: 1½ hours

2 tbsp butter

115g/4oz/scant ⅔ cup pudding rice, rinsed and drained

1½ tbsp good-quality lemon curd

500ml/17fl oz/generous 2 cups whole milk

50g/1¾oz/¼ cup caster/ granulated sugar

300ml/10½fl oz/1¼ cups double/heavy cream

1 tbsp soft thyme leaves, pulled off the stalks

6–7 juniper berries, lightly crushed

grated zest of ½ lemon

a few amaretto biscuits

Preheat the oven to 150°C/300°F/Gas 2 and grease a large ovenproof dish with half the butter.

Mix the rice, lemon curd, milk, sugar, cream, thyme leaves, juniper berries and lemon zest together and pour it into the prepared dish. Dot the mixture with the remaining butter and bake for 1½ hours until just set but still creamy. Serve hot or cold with amaretto biscuits.

A Thai goodbye

Serves: 4
Prep: 5 minutes, plus soaking
Cook: 1 hour

The insatiable appeal of Thai food never fails to stagger me. I have a local Thai all-you-can-gorge-on buffet. There, I regularly put away my own weight in sticky rice, in the manner of a Mrs Ko Samui Creosote. As I attempt to stagger home, past the afterthought of a dessert refrigerator, these coconut creamed diamonds of Bangkok wink suggestively at me ... just a wafer-thin moment later and I'm back at the table.

75g/2½oz/heaped ⅓ cup Thai fragrant rice
350ml/12fl oz/1½ cups coconut milk
150ml/5fl oz/⅔ cup single/ light cream
50g/1¾oz/¼ cup palm or caster/granulated sugar
1 tsp black sesame seeds
fresh fruit

Soak the rice overnight in 175ml/6fl oz/¾ cup water. Line a roasting pan with non-stick baking parchment.

Blitz the rice and soaking water together in a food processor until the mixture is runny with the rice grains broken, but not a paste.

Heat the coconut milk and cream in a separate non-stick frying pan over a medium heat. As the mixture approaches boiling point, add your rice mixture. Turn the heat to very low for 10 minutes, stirring constantly, then add the sugar. This mixture needs to cook for a further 15 minutes and you are aiming for a thick, creamy consistency.

Pour the rice mixture into the roasting pan and spread evenly to about 1cm/½in depth. Allow to cool, then chill in the refrigerator until the mixture is firm.

Cut the firm mixture into diamonds using a non-serrated knife. Sprinkle with the black sesame seeds and serve with any fresh fruit.

The ultimate rice hit

Rice exists at a whole remarkable level in Thai cuisine. As in many Asian cuisines, rice is at the heart of any Thai meal. The word for rice and food are the same in the Thai language: *khao*. The verb to eat is the same as to 'eat rice'.

The most famous Thai rice is the lauded and sweet aromatic jasmine rice. This grows in abundance in Thailand's central plains. This well-tempered, non-glutinous grain is used widely in fried rice dishes and in the congees, or savoury soups.

The other well-known Thai rice is the sticky rice, which for me holds an entirely unique charm. It operates in its very form so differently to the separate grains of steamed or boiled rice, behaving like a hefty sponge. It is heavy, cloying and rather unashamed at how poor its attempt to absorb sauce really is. This is why I love it. For me, Thai sticky rice is the ultimate rice hit. It does not behave as a tame accompaniment but as a shameless spoilsport. Flopped out of a plastic bag, it does not even change its shape for you. One has to wrestle it into submission. I never knew rice could be so exciting.

In its dessert form, sticky rice is at its best. I recall lurking around street stalls in Bangkok and savouring the sticky rice dishes topped with caramelized roasted grated coconut, as well as the rices cooked with banana, coconut and sugar.

And as if the glutinous rice was not weight enough, I remember a dish called *khao niao ping* served at a late-night Thai food market. Sticky rice was mixed with coconut milk, banana and taro, wrapped in banana leaf and grilled over a charcoal fire for a long while. It stayed with me, physically and emotionally, for a long time.

Scotch bonnet chocolate button risotto

Serves: 4
Prep: 10 minutes
Cook: 25 minutes

You can raise your eyebrows all you like, but my girls love me for this breach of culinary etiquette. I see it as a healing dish. I'm sure many a family rift is forgiven over a pan of melted chocolate. To really pimp it up, I have added just a touch of chilli. The smoked, buttery edge that the fried Scotch bonnet provides works beautifully in sweet dishes such as this – especially with chocolate.

2 tbsp unsalted butter

¼ tsp finely chopped Scotch bonnet chilli

175g/6oz/scant 1 cup risotto rice, rinsed and drained

600ml/21fl oz/2½ cups whole milk

75g/2½oz/½ cup chocolate buttons

50g/1¾oz/¼ cup caster/ granulated sugar

a pinch of ground cinnamon

60ml/2fl oz/¼ cup double/ heavy cream, plus extra to decorate

2 tbsp grated dark chocolate, to decorate

Melt the butter in a non-stick saucepan over a medium heat. Add the chilli and fry for a couple of minutes. Add the rice to the pan and stir briefly to coat in the butter.

Add the milk and bring to the boil, then reduce the heat to low and simmer for 20 minutes, stirring occasionally. You are waiting for the rice to become very soft.

Now stir in the chocolate buttons, sugar and cinnamon. Keep stirring over a low heat until the chocolate has melted. Remove from the heat and stir in the cream. Serve decorated with another swirl of cream and dark chocolate shavings.

Mulled pineapple & rum rice pudding

Serves: 4
Prep: 20 minutes, plus soaking
Cook: 2 hours

This has an almost Caribbean twist. I first made it with loads of sultanas/golden raisins which was lovely, heavy and toffee-like in its finish. The dish naturally called for pineapple, in my view, to brighten it and punctuate the sweet cloy with pineapple punch.

4 tbsp dark rum

75g/2½oz/heaped ½ cup sultanas/golden raisins

1 tbsp salted butter

75g/2½oz/heaped ⅓ cup pudding rice, rinsed and drained

½ small fresh pineapple, peeled, cored and finely diced

½ tsp ground cinnamon

3 whole cloves

a grating of fresh nutmeg

1 strip of pared lemon zest

½ tsp vanilla extract

90g/3¼oz/scant ½ cup demerara sugar

a pinch of salt

400g/14oz can evaporated milk made up to 600ml/ 21fl oz/2½ cups with water

150ml/5fl oz/scant ⅔ cup single/light cream

Warm the rum in a pan and pour it over the sultanas/golden raisins. Leave them to soak for at least 3 hours or preferably overnight.

Preheat the oven to 150°C/300°F/gas 2 and grease a soufflé dish lightly with a little of the butter.

Wash the rice thoroughly, then drain. Pour into the soufflé dish. Add the pineapple, spices, lemon zest, vanilla, rum and sultanas/golden raisins and stir around so that they are evenly distributed. Add 2 tablespoons of the sugar to the dish with a pinch of salt. Pour on the diluted evaporated milk and the cream and stir gently.

Dot the surface of the rice with the remaining butter and sprinkle with the remaining sugar, then bake for 2 hours.

Leave to cool for 30 minutes, then serve warm or leave to cool completely and serve cold, instructing your guests to eat around the spice shrapnel.

Hob-top spiced rice pudding

Serves: 4
Prep: 10 minutes, plus soaking
Cook: 35 minutes

This is a very popular Indian dessert. My mother would shamelessly kick-start this pudding by frying the spices and rice in clarified butter. In a nod to cardiologists, I use unsalted butter. I have to concede that this buttery beginning is critical to achieving the final nutty sweetness of the pudding. Using whole spices actually gives a gentle aroma. If you want a really spicy punch, use ground versions of the spices, once again frying them in the butter to ensure their aromatic oils are properly released to their full pimping potential. This pudding works best with basmati, not pudding rice.

100g/3½oz/scant ½ cup white basmati rice, rinsed and drained

2 tbsp unsalted butter or clarified butter

1 cinnamon stick

1 whole star anise

1 litre/35fl oz/4⅓ cups whole milk

300ml/10½fl oz/scant 1¼ cups single/light cream

4 tbsp light brown sugar

¼ tsp ground cardamom

1 tbsp flaked/slivered almonds

Soak the rice in hot water for 10 minutes to prime the grains for better absorbency. Rinse and drain.

Heat the butter in a heavy-based saucepan over a medium heat and drop in the cinnamon stick and star anise. Toss the spices in the butter, then add the rice. Allow the warm spiced butter to coat the grains, gently stirring, for 1 minute.

Add the milk, cream, sugar and cardamom and simmer over a low heat, stirring occasionally, for at least 30 minutes until the pudding becomes creamy but the grains retain a little shape.

Meanwhile, toast the almonds in a dry frying pan set over a medium heat, stirring, for 1–2 minutes until golden.

Serve the pudding warm or chilled, sprinkled with the toasted almonds.

Caramel peach congee brûlée

The triple comfort whammy of musky rice, creamy coconut and floral vanilla mediate with the fragrant freshness of the peach beautifully in this dish. Caramelizing the fruit in this way makes for a warmly sweet alternative to the hospital-ward, boiled-to-anaemia peach.

Serves: 4
Prep: 20 minutes, plus soaking
Cook: 45 minutes

100g/3½oz/heaped ½ cup Thai fragrant rice or any short-grain rice
800ml/28fl oz/3½ cups coconut milk
3 tbsp soft brown sugar
a pinch of salt
2 drops of vanilla extract

THE CARAMELIZED PEACH
3 peaches, skinned and pitted
2 tbsp salted butter
30g/1oz/2½ tbsp muscovado/soft brown sugar

THE TOPPING
8 tbsp caster/granulated sugar

Soak the rice in cold water for 4 hours or overnight, then rinse and drain.

Put all the main ingredients in a heavy-based saucepan and bring to the boil, then turn the heat down to low and simmer gently until you have a good thick porridge, stirring occasionally to prevent sticking. This will take about 30 minutes. Once the grains are cooked through, remove from the heat.

Set a strainer over a bowl and cut the skinned peaches into pieces over the strainer, so their juice collects in the bowl.

Heat the butter in a non-stick frying pan over a medium heat. When it is hot but not smoking, add the peach pieces and sauté them until they sizzle and their juices reduce and begin to thicken, which should take 2–3 minutes.

Sprinkle the muscovado/soft brown sugar over them and sauté until the juices further thicken and the sugar caramelizes slightly, about 1 minute. You may want to increase the heat under the pan to medium-high. Allow the peaches to cook, shaking the pan occasionally, until the juices are very thick, which will take a minute or so.

Just before serving, stir the caramelized peaches into the congee. Spoon the mixture into four heatproof ramekins, then sprinkle 2 tablespoons caster/granulated sugar evenly over the surface of each congee brûlée. While the sugar is still dry, immediately caramelize with a chefs' blow-torch, or by placing the ramekins under a hot grill/broil until the sugar bubbles and turns golden brown.

Banana batter pillows

Don't be expecting a sticky toffee gravity to this dessert – this is an Indonesian steamed pudding. It is light and pale and is beautifully delicate. It seems in the heat and colour of the Indonesian sun, there is no aversion to such subtlety. The banana and coconut reach up out of the pale and pillowy in a soft caress. I add a caramelized honey sauce, more to the dish than the dessert. The white crockery of the West can be the bane of the deathly pale dessert. One understands why banana leaves are all the rage in the East.

Serves: 4
Prep: 25 minutes
Cook: 30 minutes

170g/6oz/heaped 1 cup rice flour
55g/2oz/heaped ½ cup cornflour/cornstarch
4 ripe bananas
700 ml/24fl oz/3 cups coconut milk
200g/7oz/1 cup soft brown sugar
a pinch of salt
175g/6oz/½ cup clear honey
100g/3½oz/scant ½ cup unsalted butter, diced
100ml/3½fl oz/scant ½ cup double/heavy or whipping cream

Blend the rice flour, cornflour and 3 of the bananas with 100ml/3½fl oz/scant ½ cup of the coconut milk. You want a smooth paste.

Heat the rest of the coconut milk in a heavy-based saucepan over a low heat, stir in half the sugar and keep stirring until it completely dissolves. Now pour in the banana blend, making sure the mixture is smooth.

Melt half the butter and brush the inside of four ramekins.

Slice the remaining banana into discs and divide among the prepared ramekins. Top with the batter. Wrap in greased foil.

Put the ramekins on a trivet in a large saucepan. Pour in boiling water to come halfway up the sides of the ramekins. Cover with a lid and cook over a low heat for 30–45 minutes, or until puddings are just set.

Meanwhile, mix the honey and remaining sugar in a small saucepan over a medium heat. Cook until lightly caramelized. Add the remaining butter and cream and simmer until smooth.

Turn out the puddings into bowls, if you like. I think they are best served with the honey sauce poured around them, but you can pour it over the top, if you prefer.

Rose rice romance

Serves: 4
Prep: 30 minutes, plus soaking
Cook: 20 minutes

An North Indian dish known as *phirni*, this is almost blancmange-like in its texture. It is a thickened rice pudding made from rice paste. *Phirni* probably travelled to India from Persia with the Mughal invaders. The Mughals knew how to enjoy themselves, building magnificent royal monuments to matters as trifling as love. Rose petals to them were rather like Shake & Vac to us. They were strewn before the royal princesses as they walked the wipe-easy marble corridors. I tell you this so that you understand the addition of rose to Eastern dishes is not a contrived opulence. It was as mundane as us reaching into the cupboard for the tinned peaches.

50g/1¾oz/heaped ¼ cup white basmati rice
1 litre/35fl oz/4⅓ cups milk
175g/6oz/heaped ¾ cup caster/granulated sugar
4–6 tbsp rose syrup (or 1–2 tbsp rose water plus an extra 1 tbsp sugar)
seeds from 3 green cardamom pods, ground (optional)
a handful of rose petals and pistachio slivers

Soak the rice in 4 tablespoons water for an hour or so.

Drain the rice and grind it to a smooth paste in a blender or food processor. Use a little of the milk to lubricate the grinding process, if you like. Once smooth, add 240ml/8fl oz/1 cup of the milk and leave the rice milk to one side.

Now bring the remaining milk and the sugar to the boil over a medium heat in a heavy-based saucepan, stirring frequently. Add the rose syrup and mix well.

Add the rice mixture and keep stirring to ensure that no lumps form. You want to achieve a smooth mix that will start to thicken. Turn the heat to medium-low and keep stirring the mixture until it starts to boil and thicken to a custard consistency. This will take 12–15 minutes.

Add the cardamom, if using, and mix well. Remove from the heat. Let the mixture cool to room temperature, stirring occasionally to reabsorb any skin that forms on the top.

Meanwhile, drizzle some of the extra rose syrup down the insides of your dessert glasses. Spoon the rice mixture into the glasses and refrigerate until ready to serve.

Sprinkle with the rose petals and the pistachios just before serving.

Fig anise-drizzled pistachio pancakes

Serves: 4
Prep: 20 minutes, plus cooling
Cook: 50 minutes

The pistachio pancake concept is a very Turkish one. This dessert is elegant, light and the flavours put me in mind of pretty, bright restaurants with golden chandeliers and white tablecloths. Many recipes for these delicate lovelies add green food colouring just to drive the pistachio point right home. This is never something I would advocate – unless you are contributing to a comedy Turkish St Patrick's Day dessert trolley.

225g/8oz/1⅔ cups cooked white basmati rice (or cook ½ cup raw rice)

60g/2¼oz/⅓ cup caster/granulated sugar

240ml/8fl oz/1 cup whole milk

300g/10½oz/2 cups rice flour

2 tsp baking powder

1 tbsp sunflower oil, plus extra for frying

175g/6oz/scant 1¼ cups pistachios, ground

THE FIG & ANISE DRIZZLE

20 dried figs

3 tbsp white wine vinegar

400ml/14fl oz/1¾ cups water

3 star anise

2.5cm/1in piece of fresh root ginger, peeled and grated

1 cinnamon stick

1 tsp sea salt

250g/9oz/1¼ cups caster/granulated sugar

Combine the rice, sugar, milk, rice flour, baking powder and oil together in a bowl and blend with an electric hand mixer for 2 minutes. Now stir in the ground pistachios, making sure they are thoroughly blended.

Grease a large frying pan or griddle and put over a medium heat. Pour a small ladleful of the batter into the frying pan and cook until the underside is golden brown. Flip the pancake over and cook until the other side is also golden brown, about 2 minutes per side. Keep the cooked pancakes warm in a low oven while you cook the remaining pancakes in the same way. You should make about 12 pancakes.

Meanwhile, put all the drizzle ingredients in a heavy-based saucepan, bring to the boil over a medium heat, then turn the heat down and simmer gently until the drizzle gains a syrupy texture. Transfer to a bowl and leave to cool. Discard the star anise and cinnamon.

Stack the pancakes and spoon over the fig and anise drizzle to serve.

Makes: 24 doughnuts
Prep: 40 minutes
Cook: 15 minutes

Korean doughnuts

So sweetly dinky and easy to down, these are strictly prescription-only. The sharp edges of dark chocolate and ginger perk them up to an almost healthy status. The filling is not that sweet and I find the sprinkling of sugar at the end is much needed. They are stunning with sweet ginger tea.

500ml/17fl oz/generous
   2 cups rapeseed/canola or
   sunflower oil for
   deep-frying
2 tbsp caster/superfine sugar
   to sprinkle on top

THE DOUGH
500g/1lb 2 oz/3⅓ cups
   glutinous rice flour or sweet
   rice flour
80g/2¾oz/⅔ cup self-
   raising/self-rising flour
¼ tsp salt
1½ tbsp butter, melted

THE GANACHE FILLING
225g/8oz dark chocolate,
   finely chopped
180ml/6fl oz/¾ cup double/
   heavy cream
1 tsp ground ginger
1 tbsp butter
2 pieces stem ginger in syrup,
   finely diced
sweet ginger tea, to serve

Start with the filling. Put the chocolate in a bowl. Put the cream and ground ginger in a saucepan and bring to the boil, then pour over the chocolate, stirring until the chocolate is smooth, then stir in the butter. If you need to warm the mixture, pour some just-boiled water into a larger bowl and put the bowl inside it, taking care not to get water in the chocolate. Stir in the stem ginger.

Now make the dough. Sift the flours into a large bowl. Add the salt, melted butter and 480ml/16fl oz/2 cups hot water. Mix all the ingredients well and knead it to make one large ball of dough, then chill.

Remove the ganache from the refrigerator, checking that it is now firm enough to spoon into solid portions. Remove a small golf ball's worth of dough and roll on your palms to make a tiny ball. The size should be enough to hold the stuffing inside. Keep the dough balls covered with a wet dish towel to prevent them drying out. Repeat to make the remaining doughnuts.

Open up the dough by pressing the rolled balls with your thumbs. Spoon ¼ or ½ teaspoon of the chocolate ganache mixture into the centre of each dough ball, then close the dough carefully around the filling. Squeeze the dough together to ensure the parcels are absolutely sealed. Put them on a baking sheet and, if you can, back in the refrigerator until you are ready to fry them.

Heat the oil in a wide-based saucepan or wok over a medium-high heat. Test the heat of the oil by dropping in a small pea-size ball of dough. It needs to bubble briskly and rise to the top of the pan, turning golden brown. Once this is achieved, carefully spoon in the doughnuts in batches of 4 or 5 and fry for a few minutes until the dough is golden brown. Gently roll the doughnuts with a metal slotted spoon while cooking to prevent them sticking together and to encourage the balls to keep their shape.

Once all the dough is cooked, roll the balls in the sugar, then leave them to cool for a few minutes before serving.

Have you eaten rice today?

Much like Thailand, rice is central to Korean cuisine, and shares the fact that the Korean word for rice (*bap*) is also used to describe meals or food in general. That's quite a preposterous position for one ingredient, when instead of asking, 'Have you had a meal?', Koreans usually ask, 'Have you eaten rice today?'

Rice is the staple food for most Koreans and, as a result, it appears at almost every meal. Although it is most usually cooked alone, it is also occasionally teamed with other grains, such as millet or barley. It is also combined with chestnuts and different kinds of beans. Rice in Korea often appears in a gruel form, which is given to the elderly and infirm.

One of Korea's most famous dishes is the *bibimbap*: a bowl of rice topped with a variety – any variety – of vegetables, meats and often a good runny egg. I had to include a recipe for Beefed-Up Bibimbap (see page 78) as I travelled to Korea just to eat my way around, and came across this fabulous dish for the first time. The heavy stone bowl hissed warningly at me in complete contradiction to the playful meeting of bright ingredients on top. I recall asking – gesticulating really – the waitress what to do. She approached with a ketchup bottle of red sweet chilli sauce and covered the whole dish in it. She then took my fine metal spoon and mashed the work of culinary art into an unsightly rice massacre. Now eat, she gestured. It was stunning. I fell in love with the crunch of the burnt rice on the bottom of the bowl, the sweetness of the chilli sauce, the reassurance of the wet egg and the utterly otiose meat. This ravaged rice dish became an obsession. Thank heavens Korean cuisine has become popular in the UK.

On another occasion, I recall stumbling, grimy and exhausted, around a street market in Jeju, when I was confronted by what the Koreans are capable of with their carbs. Their delightful, oozing, rice-flour doughnuts provided me with the ultimate shoppers' stress relief and the inspiration for my sweet concoction, opposite.

Lemongrass lemon cheesecake

This is the cookie-dough ice cream of the cheesecake world. Rice heft straddles cream weight. The lemongrass and lemon breeze in to bring fragrant levity to this uncompromising coupling.

Serves: 6
Prep: 45 minutes, plus chilling
Cook: 1 hour 15 minutes

115g/4oz/scant ⅔ cup Thai fragrant rice, rinsed and drained
1 lemongrass stalk
500ml/17fl oz/generous 2 cups whole milk
100g/3½oz/½ cup caster/ granulated sugar
a few cardamom pods
1 bay leaf
150ml/5fl oz/scant ⅔ cup whipping cream
1 tbsp freshly squeezed lemon juice
3 eggs, separated

THE LEMON TOPPING
120ml/4fl oz/½ cup double/ heavy cream
75g/2½oz cup low-fat soft cheese or Quark
grated zest and juice of ½ lemon
1–2 tbsp caster/granulated sugar
shavings of good dark chocolate

Put the rice in a saucepan and cover it with water. Bring to the boil over a medium-high heat, then boil for 3 minutes. Drain, then return it to a dry pan.

Crush the lemongrass with the back of a knife, ensuring that the fibrous tissue is displayed. Add the milk, half the sugar, the cardamom pods, bay leaf and lemongrass to the rice in the pan and bring to the boil. Turn down the heat and simmer for 20 minutes. Leave the mixture to cool. Remove the cardamom pods, lemongrass and bay leaf. Transfer this mixture to a large bowl.

Preheat the oven to 180°C/350°F/Gas 4 and grease and line a 23cm/9in round deep cake pan.

Beat the cream, lemon juice and egg yolks into the rice mixture with the remaining sugar.

Whisk the egg whites separately in a clean, grease-free bowl, until they form soft peaks. Fold them into the rice mixture, then spoon the mixture into the prepared pan and bake for 45–50 minutes. You are waiting for it to rise and become golden. The mixture might feel soft to the touch in the middle but fear not, it firms up as it cools. Chill overnight, then remove the cake from the pan.

For the topping, whip the cream until stiff, then fold in the soft cheese, lemon zest, lemon juice and sugar. Heap this mixture on top of the cake and decorate with shavings of dark chocolate and a sprinkling of lemon zest.

White chocolate orange cereal stickies

Serves: 4
Prep: 20 minutes,
plus setting
Cook: 10 minutes

Those in the know say that good white chocolate has a natural lemon hint to it. White chocolate for me, however, conjures precocious blonde cowboys and the sweet, cloying condensed milk hit on the trek back from my 1970s childhood sweetshop. The elegance of the orange and lime zest make this a very grown-up, respectable affair. Golden syrup is used as the happy lubricant but marshmallows take me back to that sunny Skelmersdale street and make the dish a heck of a lot more fun to make.

2 tbsp butter, plus extra for greasing
175g/6oz/scant 4½ cups miniature marshmallows
45g/1½oz/⅓ cup white chocolate chips
grated zest of 1 navel orange
1 tbsp freshly squeezed orange juice
70g/2½oz/3 cups crispy rice cereal
non-stick cooking spray
grated zest of ½ small lime
50g/1¾oz bar of white chocolate, grated or shaved

Melt the butter over a low heat in a heavy-based saucepan. Add the marshmallows and stir until completely melted. Remove from the heat. Stir in the white chocolate chips and most of the orange zest and juice. Add the crispy rice cereal and stir until all the ingredients are well combined.

Grease an 18cm/7in square baking pan and a rubber spatula with non-stick cooking spray. Pour the mixture into the tray and spread with the buttered spatula. It will be quite thick. Press flat with baking parchment and refrigerate for at least 2 hours.

Sprinkle with shaved or grated white chocolate, the reserved orange zest and the lime zest before cutting into sticky rectangles.

Raspberry rice cake

Serves: 6–8
Prep: 45 minutes
Cook: 20 minutes

My childhood best friend suffers from coeliac disease, as do other members of her family. This exposed me to a childhood filled with inventive and delicious rice cakes. This one was a favourite on the wheat-avoidant dessert trolley. The almond lilt and the raspberry bite work beautifully in the dense, moist cake base. I actually love it warm – fresh from the Coleraine farmhouse oven in Northern Ireland, where I first tasted it – but a cooled, creamy version is a rich, elegant variation.

THE RICE CAKE

butter, for greasing
100g/3½oz/heaped ½ cup
   pudding or short-grain rice,
   rinsed and drained
350ml/12fl oz/1½ cups
   whole milk
a pinch of ground cinnamon
2 eggs
8 tbsp granulated sugar
110g/3¾oz/heaped 1 cup
   ground almonds

THE RASPBERRY TOPPING

450g/1lb fresh raspberries
1 tbsp caster/granulated
   sugar

Preheat the oven to 180°C/350°F/Gas 4. Butter a 23cm/9in round baking dish and line with baking parchment.

Put the rice in a heavy-based saucepan. Add the milk and cinnamon, bring to the boil over a high heat, then turn the heat down and simmer over a medium heat for 30 minutes, or until the milk has been absorbed by the rice. Leave to cool.

Beat the eggs and sugar thoroughly in a clean glass bowl. You are looking for a frothy head to develop. Now add the almonds and stir in well.

Add this egg mixture to the rice and stir together well, then pour the whole mixture into the baking dish. Now drop half of the fresh raspberries into the mixture, at equal intervals around the baking dish.

Bake in the middle of the oven for 30 minutes or so until the cake begins to turn golden brown and firm to the touch.

Remove from the oven and allow to cool slightly. Put a large plate on top of the baking dish and turn the cake upside down onto the plate. Remove the baking parchment and allow the cake to cool

Once cooled and just before serving, spread the whipped cream over the cake and, using your best village fête efforts, arrange the remaining raspberries on top to give the cake a summery voice.

Hungarian lemon & raisin rice cake

Serves: 6–8
Prep: 35 minutes
Cook: 1 hour 20 minutes

This cake is supposed to be fluffy and light. It is also supposed to be served cold, with the lemon zest brightening the sweet, moist softness, but in truth, it very rarely makes it to the cold stage in our household.

2 tbsp salted butter, plus extra for greasing
1 litre/35fl oz/4⅓ cups whole milk
200g/7oz/heaped 1 cup pudding or long-grain white rice, rinsed and drained
a pinch of salt
4 large eggs, separated
75g/2½oz/heaped ⅓ cup granulated sugar
150g/5½oz/heaped 1 cup raisins
grated zest of ½ lemon
cream (optional)

Preheat the oven to 180°C/350°F/gas 4 and lightly butter a 23cm/9in shallow springform cake pan or ceramic dish.

Bring the milk, rice and salt to a simmer over a medium heat in a heavy-based saucepan, then turn the heat down to low and simmer for about 30 minutes. You are waiting for the rice milk to become creamy and the grains to be tender. Remove from the heat and stir in the butter. Leave to cool down to room temperature.

In a clean glass bowl, mix the egg yolks with the sugar, raisins and lemon zest. Stir this mixture into the rice pudding.

In a large mixing bowl, whisk the egg whites until they form stiff peaks. Gently stir one-quarter of the whites into the rice and yolk mixture, then gently fold in the rest of the whites, making sure the air is not knocked out of the mixture.

Transfer this mixture to the prepared cake pan and bake in the middle of the oven for about 45 minutes until the top is golden brown.

Remove from the oven and leave to cool. Turn out, sprinkle with sugar and serve cold or chilled with cream or without. Alternatively, serve warm straight from the dish.

Pear & almond rice flour tart

Serves: 6–8
Prep: 15 minutes
Cook: 35 minutes

A very French, very guest house in the Dordogne, late-supper slice. Wherever you are, this should take you there. I use pears, they use pears. You could go plums, or crystallized ginger or berries. Just get the rice flan technique under your belt and let your whim take you where it will.

115g/4oz/½ cup unsalted butter, plus extra for greasing
115g/4oz/heaped ½ cup caster/granulated sugar
2 eggs
4 drops of almond extract
75g/2½oz/heaped ½ cup self-raising/self-rising flour
50g/1¾oz/heaped ¼ cup ground rice
4 ripe pears
1 tsp lemon juice
2 tbsp soft brown sugar
25g/1oz/2 tbsp flaked/ slivered almonds
jam, cream or custard

Preheat the oven to 180°C/350°F/Gas 4 and lightly grease a 25cm/10in cake pan or flan dish.

Cream the butter and caster/granulated sugar together In a large glass bowl until light and fluffy. Beat in the eggs and almond extract, then fold in the flour and ground rice. Spoon this mixture into the prepared pan.

Peel and quarter the pears and toss them in the lemon juice and brown sugar. Arrange them in the pan and gently press them into the cake mixture. Bake for 10 minutes, then sprinkle the flaked/slivered almonds on top of the flan and bake for a further 25 minutes, or until the top is a beautiful golden brown. Err on the side of brown!

Serve with a dollop of good jam, fresh cream or custard.

Makes: 16 biscuits
Prep: 20 minutes,
plus chilling
Cook: 20 minutes

Lavender lovers' shortbread

Unashamedly romantic. The brusque, masculine coarseness imparted by the rice flour is hijacked by the feminine stumble into lavender. The rice flour does give these shortbreads a brisk texture. However, to achieve that real summer evening, tea-in-the-garden, Darcy drifting through the delphiniums moment, ladies, it is in lavender we trust. Heart-shaped cutters please! To make vanilla sugar, immerse a vanilla pod in a jar of sugar and leave for at least a week before using.

225g/8oz/1 cup unsalted butter, softened

125g/4½oz/scant ⅔ cup vanilla sugar, plus a little extra for sprinkling

50g/1¾oz/⅓ cup rice flour

300g/10½oz/2¼ cups plain/all-purpose flour, plus extra for dusting

2 tsp dried edible lavender flowers

¼ tsp dried thyme

Cream together the butter and sugar in a large mixing bowl.

Sift in the flours and add the lavender and thyme. Mix gently until the consistency is that of breadcrumbs. Flour your hands and work the mixture into a paste.

Knead the mixture on a lightly floured work surface until you achieve a smooth dough. This will need to be wrapped in cling film/plastic wrap and go into the refrigerator for 15 minutes to firm up. While you are waiting, line two large baking sheets with baking parchment.

Roll out the chilled dough on a lightly floured surface into a 5mm /¼in thick sheet and cut out the biscuits with a heart-shaped cutter. Put the biscuits onto the baking sheets and sprinkle with some of the extra sugar.

Leave to chill in the refrigerator for a further 20 minutes. Preheat the oven to 180°C/350°F/Gas 4.

Bake for 15–20 minutes. You are looking for a delicate golden finish. Put the baked biscuits on a cooling rack and sprinkle with a final dusting of sugar. Allow to cool completely before serving.

Black rice

This is a short-grain rice that tastes mildly nutty, similar in its cooking behaviour to brown rice. This slightly sticky rice is great in desserts – creamy, yielding and dramatically occult. It works fantastically in my Black Rice & Coconut Sorbet (see opposite). The fact that it's also known as 'forbidden rice' makes it instantly enticing. ('Forbidden' to anyone who was not a Chinese noble ... which takes the charm out of it a little.)

Then there is the burgeoning research suggesting this rice is the ultimate superfood. Better for you than blueberries, say the blasphemers. Full of anthocyanin and vitamin E, antioxidants, fibre and amino acids, it's not just a pretty face.

And it does have a pretty face. It turns deep purple when cooked and so is often deployed as a dramatic dessert rice in the East. It carries the same flavour as brown rice. As a sticky rice, it's essentially filling and rich – great to tart up lacklustre, anaemic dishes with flavour and contrast. It is not to be confused with his cousin, that rakish dandy, wild rice. This is a grain that it is advisable to soak if you have time.

How to cook plain black rice

* Use 1 cup of rice to 2 cups of water (190g/6¾oz rice to 480ml/16fl oz water).

* Soak the rice in cold water for at least 2 hours, even overnight, then drain.

* Put the rice in a colander and rinse under cold running water until the water runs clear. Leave to drain.

* Put the rice in a saucepan and add the water. Bring to the boil, then boil vigorously for about 30 minutes (if soaked) or about 1 hour (unsoaked), uncovered, until almost dry with a dimpled surface.

* Cover tightly, remove from the heat and leave to stand for 20 minutes.

Black rice & coconut sorbet

Serves: 4
Prep: 20 minutes, plus soaking and freezing
Cook: 50 minutes

A glutinous black-rice pudding sorbet – a strange sentence, I know. Emotionally, I love the dissonance this dish creates. The Chinese call this 'forbidden rice'. As an Indian, rice should represent the epitome of white, musky, purity. This black rice, to us Indians, is subversive. It has flavour. It has body. This dish is sweet. It's a Black Sabbath and One Direction playlist ... and I love it.

THE RICE

200g/7oz/heaped 1 cup black rice

1 tsp vanilla extract

¼ vanilla pod/bean, split lengthways

1 tbsp clear honey

1 egg white

1 lemon, sliced or a sliver of pineapple

THE SAUCE

400ml/14fl oz/1¾ cups coconut milk

100g/3½oz/½ cup caster/ granulated sugar

2 tbsp lemon juice

1 tbsp dark rum

As is usual with black rice, a little bit of preparation is required to give this dish the love it needs. Weigh out the black rice, then rinse it 2–3 times under a cold tap until the water runs clear. Put it in a bowl, cover with cold water and leave it in the refrigerator overnight (or for at least 8 hours).

Once you are ready to cook, drain off the soaking water from the rice and transfer it to a saucepan. Add 480ml/17fl oz/2 cups lukewarm water, the vanilla extract and vanilla pod/bean. Bring this to the boil, then put a lid on the pan, reduce the heat to low and simmer very gently for about 20 minutes until the water is nearly all absorbed and the rice has softened.

Stir through the honey, then remove the pan from the heat and leave to cool.

While the rice is cooking, combine all the sauce ingredients in a saucepan and bring to the boil over a medium-high heat. As soon as the sauce hits a rolling boil, take it off the heat and leave it to cool to 5–8°C/41–46°F or at least room temperature.

Once the rice and sauce have cooled, whisk the egg white until it forms soft peaks, then fold this through the sauce. Finally fold in the rice and any juices/liquids that have leached out into the pan. Freeze the entire mixture for 1 hour, then use a hand blender to break up some of the rice. We don't want puréed rice, just to break down some of the grains. Return the mixture to the freezer for 30 minutes, then repeat the mixing process. Don't worry if at first the rice sits at the bottom of your container. As the sorbet freezes and you stir and agitate it, the rice mixture will spread throughout the dish, adding little granules of texture to break up the smooth coconut sorbet. Continue the mixing and freezing every half an hour until a sorbet consistency is achieved. This can take 3–5 hours.

Serve scoops of sorbet in a glass or ramekin, topped with a slice of lemon or a sliver of pineapple. Not only do these sit nicely with the coconut flavours, but the colours nicely complement the gentle purple sorbet.

Ricotta, raspberry & basil frozen custard rice

Serves: 4-6
Prep: 45 minutes, plus cooling and freezing
Cook: 15 minutes

This recipe is really a light, low-fat ice cream of sorts. I fell in love with the basil and rock salt combination when I first came across it in the Michelin-starred *Fraîche*. So haunt me then, I said, and have sought to graft it onto any and every vehicle I can. This sour raspberry custard carries it well.

500g/1lb 2oz/4 cups fresh raspberries

150g/5½oz/¾ cup caster/granulated sugar

1 handful of fresh basil, leaves and stalks finely chopped as ribbon-like as you can

75g/2½oz/heaped ⅓ cup risotto rice, preferably Arborio, rinsed and drained

250ml/9fl oz/generous 1 cup whole milk

250g/9oz/heaped 1 cup ricotta cheese

500g/1lb 2oz good-quality fresh custard

1 tsp rock salt crystals, to garnish (optional)

Push the raspberries through a sieve/fine mesh strainer over a large bowl. Stir in 50g/1¾oz/heaped ¼ cup of the sugar and the chopped basil and leave it to stand for 30 minutes at room temperature, stirring occasionally to dissolve the sugar.

Bring the rice and milk to the boil in a saucepan over a medium heat, stirring, then reduce the heat to low. Cover and cook for 10 minutes, stirring halfway, until the rice is just cooked. Leave to one side for 15 minutes.

Dissolve the remaining sugar in 100ml/3½fl oz/scant ½ cup water in a small pan over a low heat, then increase the heat and boil for 1 minute. Leave to cool.

Beat the ricotta, custard, raspberry and basil mixture and sugar syrup in a bowl until smooth. Fold in the cooked rice. Pour the mixture into a freezer container and leave in the freezer until the sides begin to solidify, which will take 2-3 hours.

Remove the ice cream from the freezer and stir to break up any ice crystals. Return to the freezer and repeat the process once more, but this time leave the ice cream until almost frozen solid, then either process quickly or scrape into a bowl and beat vigorously to break up the larger ice crystals. Return to the freezer and leave to freeze fully.

Transfer from the freezer to the refrigerator 30-45 minutes before serving, to soften. To serve, scoop into serving glasses and decorate with a sprig of basil and the slightest sprinkling of rock salt to get them talking.

Hibiscus & lime sherbet

Serves: 4
Prep: 5 minutes

The sherbet is an Eastern quick-cooling fix. It is a rich, luxurious drink that is chilled and served over ice to ameliorate the bulk blow. I find rice milk lightens the sweet density. The rhubarb-raspberry flavours of the hibiscus, along with the sharp prod of the lime, give the palate plenty to think about after a light summertime meal. The hibiscus flower syrup is found in many supermarkets now, beautifully stored in jars with the flowers floating in the liquid. Save the flowers for your glass of sparkling wine, and watch them unfurl amongst the bubbles.

500ml/17fl oz/generous
  2 cups rice milk
2 tbsp double/heavy cream
140g/5oz/scant 1½ cups
  finely ground almonds
60g/2¼oz/½ cup icing/
  confectioner's sugar
4 tbsp hibiscus flower syrup
grated zest and juice of 1
  lime
ice

Combine the rice milk, cream, ground almonds, icing/confectioners' sugar, hibiscus syrup and lime juice in a blender, and blitz until thoroughly mixed and smooth, about 1 minute.

Serve as a long drink over ice with a little grated lime zest on top.

Index

Acknowledgements

Thank you, Jan and Borra, my agents at DML, for taking a punt on me on the strength of your gut feeling and a grainy YouTube video. Also Grace and Becci, at Nourish, for giving this book the dignity of their focus and passion; to Georgie, Lara, Aya and Linda, for making it look great; and to Wendy, thank you for being the warmest, most intelligent and patient editor that any author could wish for.

My love for food and my obsession with feeding those I love comes from my mother, father, Monmon and AK. They are the ones I phone first thing in the morning, mid afternoon and last thing at night, when inevitably we discuss the issues of food and family with grit and gusto. Latterly, Anyu came into my life with her Hungarian kitchen wizardry, and I thank God that he thought my life was not yet studded with enough fantastic foodies. I wrote this book for India, Tia, Shona, Mirren and Nayan so that these priceless kernels of food knowledge, gleaned from these precious elders, can be theirs forever.

Night upon night, my family watched and fended for themselves whilst I immersed myself in the world and wonders of rice. Without the enthusiasm, support and understanding of Tia, India and Zoltan – here and in every aspect of my life – I would live forever in the shadows of perhaps and wondering. For the kindest husband who ever lived and my incredible girls, God, I am so grateful.